INSTANT PROFIT

Other Books in the Instant Success Series

Successful Franchising by Bradley J. Sugars

The Real Estate Coach by Bradley J. Sugars

Billionaire in Training by Bradley J. Sugars

Instant Cashflow by Bradley J. Sugars

Instant Sales by Bradley J. Sugars

Instant Leads by Bradley J. Sugars

Instant Promotions by Bradley J. Sugars

Instant Repeat Business by Bradley J. Sugars

Instant Team Building by Bradley J. Sugars

Instant Systems by Bradley J. Sugars

Instant Referrals by Bradley J. Sugars

Instant Advertising by Bradley J. Sugars

The Business Coach by Bradley J. Sugars

INSTANT PROFIT

BRADLEY J. SUGARS

McGraw-Hill

New York   Chicago   San Francisco   Lisbon   London
Madrid   Mexico City   Milan   New Delhi   San Juan
Seoul   Singapore   Sydney   Toronto

The McGraw·Hill Companies

1 2 3 4 5 6 7 8 9 0   FGR/FGR   0 9 8 7 6 5

ISBN 0-07-146668-1

This publication is designed to provide accurate and authoritative information in regard to the subject matter covered. It is sold with the understanding that neither the author nor the publisher is engaged in rendering legal, accounting, or other professional service. If legal advice or other expert assistance is required, the services of a competent professional person should be sought.
—From a Declaration of Principles jointly adopted by Committee of the American Bar Association and a Committee of Publishers.

McGraw-Hill books are available at special quantity discounts to use as premiums and sales promotions, or for use in corporate training programs. For more information, please write to the Director of Special Sales, McGraw-Hill Professional, Two Penn Plaza, New York, NY 10121-2298. Or contact your local bookstore.

Instant profit / Bradley J. Sugars.
    p. cm.
ISBN 0-07-146668-1 (alk. paper)
1. Small business—Management.   2. Profit.   I. Title.
HD2341.S84 2006
658.02'2—dc22

                                              2005025347

Dedicated to all Action Business Coaches,

leaders in every sense of the word.

 CONTENTS

Bradley J. Sugars

▌ Introduction

One of the most common questions I get asked by business owners from all over the world is how they can improve their profits. Profit is the one thing they all want more of.

And that's understandable, because *profit* is the very thing they are all in business for. This reminds me of something that Samual Gompers said back in 1908. It was very true then and it still is today. He said the worst crime against working people is a company that fails to operate at a profit. Isn't that interesting?

Anyway, my answer to these business owners is simple, and it always comes as something of a surprise. I always tell them that profit is the one thing they can't get more of.

That's right, I'll run this past you again. Profit is something business owners simply can't get more of. But they certainly can influence their bottom lines by working on, and improving, the variables that contribute towards the profitability of their businesses.

Confused? Then read on. You should view your business in terms of its five separate and distinct areas. You need to break your business down into a simple schematic of what the business looks like. It doesn't matter where you are, what you do, or how big your business is, the schematic still applies. I call it the Business Chassis. When you truly understand how a business works, you'll realize that profit's a factor that is the result of other variables and can't be directly altered in isolation. The same applies for customers and turnover.

You can't get more customers. But you can increase the number of leads you get and improve your conversion rate, which together will result in more customers. Similarly, you can't get a higher turnover without improving the number of transactions each customer makes as well as the average dollar amount they spend.

Let me show you what I'm talking about by means of a diagram. You can read more about this in my book *Instant Cashflow*.

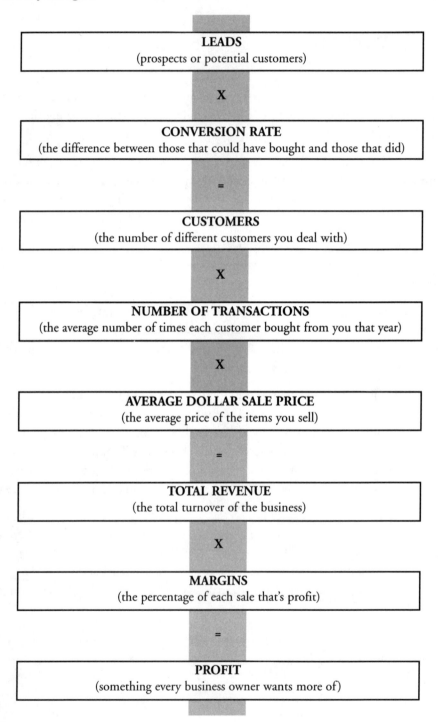

LEADS
(prospects or potential customers)

X

CONVERSION RATE
(the difference between those that could have bought and those that did)

=

CUSTOMERS
(the number of different customers you deal with)

X

NUMBER OF TRANSACTIONS
(the average number of times each customer bought from you that year)

X

AVERAGE DOLLAR SALE PRICE
(the average price of the items you sell)

=

TOTAL REVENUE
(the total turnover of the business)

X

MARGINS
(the percentage of each sale that's profit)

=

PROFIT
(something every business owner wants more of)

Understand this: The items that come after an = sign can't be directly influenced. But the items that come after an X can.

Profit has to do with the last part of the Business Chassis—the Average Dollar Sale (which affects Turnover) and Margins. Activities designed to improve Turnover and Margins have a direct effect on Profit. They include things like pricing policy, discounting, up-selling, and controlling expenditure, and I'm sure most of you will be familiar with these, at least in general terms. But there are other, less obvious, activities that are just as important. Things like cutting down on overtime, reviewing the size of your team, reducing unnecessary layers of management, and decreasing your stock levels, to mention but a few.

You'll learn all you need to know about these different strategies by reading this book. It's designed as a road map to profitability. Follow the general gist of the book or implement the strategies as they are; the choice is yours. But like everything in life, if you want to succeed, to truly succeed, you have to take responsibility for your actions. Don't be like most people and leave everything to chance. Be proactive and determine your own destiny. Choose to be a *victor* and not a *victim*.

So, congratulations on deciding to take proactive steps to improve the profitability of your business by buying this book. By concentrating on first things first, you'll set in motion a chain of activities that will generate more profit for your business. I personally guarantee it.

This book is designed to give you the inside track on everything you need to know about bumping up your business. It aims to provide you with an *instant* guide on how to improve your profitability. Once you've read the book, you'll know precisely what it takes to make your business much more profitable than it is now.

This book is the next step in your success story. From this moment on, you won't have to dream about the day when you're recognized as a leader in your field. You'll know precisely what to do to make it a reality. You'll also know exactly how to go about generating more profit than you ever dreamed possible. It's not rocket science; once you've read this book you'll realize it's nothing more than good, old-fashioned, common sense. And that's the beauty of it, because it means that you don't need to be a financial wizard, or even a qualified accountant, to make this happen. Anyone can do it.

So what are you waiting for? Dive straight in, read this book, and begin turning your business around. It's that simple.

■ How to Use This Book

This book is divided into different parts, one for each of the major business areas I'll be discussing. Pick the area that interests you most, jump straight in, and begin working through the steps outlined. Each covers important aspects relating to the various areas that will have a direct bearing on your profits.

Of course, some ideas will be more relevant to your business than others; it all depends on your particular situation. But don't discard out of hand those that you think are not relevant. Give them consideration and think creatively. Perhaps they could be adapted to produce a unique, tailor-made solution that perfectly suits your needs. Perhaps you can develop a variation on a theme. Perhaps you will come up with something entirely unique. The important thing is to approach this with an open mind. Don't say to yourself that you know everything about running your business, so nobody can teach you anything new. I know the temptation to do this is great.

Let me give you a very good real-life example of what I mean. DK Design Kitchens is a Sydney-based business whose team members thought they were going along just nicely, until they came across Greg Albert, one of my Business Coaches. This is what Pernille Lemming, one of the company's owners, has to say:

"At the time of meeting Greg Albert from *Action*, the company had grown to 15 employees. Our sales were OK—though not great—but workflow and speed in the factory were in disarray. It is safe to say our team was not happy, and we had a lot of "reworks" and some unhappy customers. When Jakob (co-owner of the company) first met Greg, he said, 'This guy can't tell me anything about selling and sales; I have been doing this for 12 years and know what to do.' However, I knew something had to change; we were working long hours, not making much profit, and had a lot of fires to put out."

After just 12 months of coaching, the company reported significant growth, with turnover up 30 percent. But perhaps more importantly, they had turned around from running at a slight loss to recording a net profit of $250,000. And all because Jakob had realized his stubborn attitude would get him nowhere. The turning point for DK Design Kitchens came when he made a conscious decision.

That's all. He decided that perhaps, just perhaps, he didn't know it all—just perhaps there is something else he could learn about running a business. Once he had opened up his mind to this possibility, things started to happen. He became receptive to new ideas, new challenges, and new opportunities. He shrugged off the silly notion that not knowing all there is to know somehow lowers his esteem in the eyes of his peers, team members, or the local business community. As soon as he did this, he became receptive to new knowledge, and his business began to transform itself. He never looked back.

So learn by this example. Open up your mind to new ways of looking at your business, to new ways of going about whatever it is you do, to new ways of earning a profit.

You might decide to implement all the great ideas explained in this book all at once. Or you might decide to implement them one at a time. But whatever you decide, the important thing is you'll no longer be blundering around in the dark, unsure whether what you're doing has a chance of nudging your profit graph northwards.

We'll begin by catching up with my mechanic Charlie, who decided it was time he began concentrating on profit. You see, he might not have much of a business brain, but he realized early on that profit is the name of the game. Follow his experiences and learn, as he did, about the dramatic results that can be obtained by implementing some of these profit-boosting strategies.

You might also be surprised at how much this exercise will reveal about your business. It may get you thinking about important issues that have never crossed your mind before. If some of this information is new to you, don't be concerned. There's never been a better time to start working on improving your knowledge base, and your bottom line.

Make sure you make notes as you go along. When you come to designing your own profit-boosting plan, you'll find it useful referring back to them. You'll find real life examples and proven ideas that, when combined with your new knowledge, will bring results.

Now it's time to get started. There is additional profit just waiting to be made. All you need is the right frame of mind and some proven profit-boosting strategies and you're in business.

■ Charlie Discovers That Profit Is King

Ever since I first started having my cars serviced at Charlie's Garage, I could tell he was more than your average mechanic. And I don't mean that in a technical sense either. He has a genuine interest in trying to get the best from the cars he looks after, but he also wants to get the best from his business.

I like that. You see, why else would you want to be in business?

Once I got to know Charlie better, he began seeking my help, and I gladly obliged. He quickly became a willing student, and the results followed. Slowly but surely he implemented strategies aimed at generating more leads for his business, converting those leads into customers, and then making sure those customers became loyal ones.

His business began to thrive and he soon needed to increase the size of his workforce. In no time at all he was running a very busy, and popular, mechanical workshop. The work kept rolling in and he quickly became known as something of a mover and shaker in the local business community.

It wasn't long before he began turning his attention to his bottom line. He wanted to pump up his profits.

It was a hot and humid morning when I pulled up outside his garage. The traffic was worse than normal. It took me an agonizing 45 minutes to crawl the short journey to his place. And strange as it may seem, I felt on top of the world. I love anything to do with profit, especially the challenge of putting in place strategies aimed at maximizing it.

I was in my element.

"Hi, Charlie. How're you doing?" I asked as he came out to greet me.

"Good to see you," he replied. "I've been so looking forward to this day, I just can't tell you."

He led me into his small but functional office and offered me a chair. From where I sat I had a very good view of the workshop.

"You couldn't fit any more cars in there if you tried," I quipped, nodding towards the window that separated the office from the workshop. "What's that bike in the far corner?"

"That's my latest toy, Brad. It's a V-Rod, you know, the latest Harley Davidson."

"Nice, very nice," I said. "It's quite different from anything they've made before, isn't it?"

"For sure, and does it go! Also, that tank is just a dummy. The real one is actually under the seat."

Charlie shared my passion for fast machinery.

"You know, having a passion for fast cars is very much like having a passion for business—you're always striving for something better. And that's what I love about it. Business is just like a game. It must be fun, you have to play by the rules to succeed, and by keeping score you have a benchmark to gauge whether you are improving or not."

"That's interesting, Brad. I've noticed before that you always refer to business as a game. That got me thinking and it certainly helped me feel better when I lost on a job, if you follow my meaning."

"That's right, Charlie. It's OK to lose every once in a while. No team can win them all, but as long as it's heading in the right direction, that's what it's all about. This applies to business as well. You need to understand that if you don't allow yourself to fail, you'll never try new things, and in business, that's not good. You need to be willing to try new strategies, some of which will work while others won't. But it's the ones that do that we're interested in. They're the ones that will produce the results you're after. You'll see what I mean in a minute."

I leaned back in my chair and let what I had just said sink in. I wanted to be sure Charlie understood that the profit a business earns is the result of other factors that interact together to produce a result.

After a few moments, I dropped my voice down an octave or two and continued.

"You need to understand this, Charlie. Profit in itself is something you can't have more of. But you can have more money from your existing customers by getting them to spend more than they usually do, and you can have more money in your pocket from the things they buy through having larger margins. Does that make sense?"

His eyes were fixed on the yellow Saab convertible that was on the hoist in the workshop. I knew he wasn't concentrating on the car, or the two mechanics who were working on it.

"So, you're telling me I can never make more profit than I am at present?"

"What I'm suggesting, Charlie, is that you simply can't have more profit on its own. Let me put it this way: If you want to see more money in your cash register at the end of each day, what do you have to do? You have to sell more, don't you? You can't just sit back and hope more money will mysteriously appear. You've got to work on the selling part of the equation if you want to end up with more in the results part—in this example, the cash register. You have to work on the first part of the equation to influence the second."

The blank expression had suddenly disappeared from his face. The penny had dropped.

"Ah, I see. That's brilliant, Brad. I see exactly what you mean. If I want more profit—and don't we all—then I need to think about the things that work together to give profit."

"Exactly. Remember back to when we talked about the Business Chassis. When we wanted to work on increasing the number of customers you had, we put in place strategies aimed at increasing the number of leads you get and ways of converting those leads—or making them buy. The result of these two variables gives you your customers."

"So are you saying that profit is the mix of getting people to spend more and increasing my margins?"

I love it when a concept sinks in.

"That's essentially it, Charlie. Or in the language of the Business Chassis, you need to work on your Average Dollar Sale and Margins to influence your Profit. It's as simple as that."

Breaking business concepts down into simple-to-understand entities always makes it easier for people to understand. It also dramatically increases the chances of improving the performance of your businesses because it forces you to begin working *on* the business instead of *in* it. And once you begin doing this, you will quickly begin reaping the benefits.

"So what we're going to do now is take a closer look at all the things you can do to increase both your Average Dollar Sale and your Margins. We'll then decide which of these are best suited to your business, and then which should be implemented."

"Sounds fantastic. Can't wait to hear what you have to say. Would you like something to drink first?"

"No thanks, Charlie. Let's dive right in."

To make things simpler, or easier to grasp, I decided to discuss Charlie's Garage in different segments according to its different functional areas.

"When it comes to profit, we'll look at it from four different standpoints, Charlie. That's because there are basically four different business areas that relate to the profit you make. They are management, sales and marketing, finance, and stock. We'll handle them one at a time."

▌ Determine Your Current Situation

Before we get down to discussing various strategies aimed at boosting your profits, there's one very important concept I need to discuss, and that's knowing where your business is from a profit point-of-view *before* you start implementing anything.

You need to know what the situation is before you attempt to change it; otherwise you'll have no idea whether you've successfully implemented change, and if you have, how much.

Understand this: If you want to get to a particular destination, you'll never know that you've arrived unless you know where you started. Make sense? For instance, if you want to increase your profitability by 25 percent, what does that actually mean? It's meaningless, unless you already know what your profitability is at the time you made that decision. If you want to drive somewhere, how would you know in which direction to head unless you knew where you started?

Before you begin implementing profit-boosting strategies, you need to conduct two surveys, one to determine exactly what your Average Dollar Sale is, and the other to determine what your Margins are.

Now it's possible you already know this. If you do, congratulations—you are something of a rarity in the business community. But if you don't, or if you are unsure, then read on.

I'm sure you're all familiar with the term stocktaking. Most businesses conduct this regularly because it's a requirement, from an accounting point-of-view. But how many take stock of other areas of their operation? Why should you confine stocktaking to that part of your business that deals predominantly with stock?

I think it's due to old-fashioned thinking; even the term stocktaking is, in my vocabulary, outmoded. That's why I don't use it. Well, not for all those other business areas that I'm now talking about anyway. You see, you should be "taking stock" of where your business is as far as all your marketing efforts are concerned. You need to know where you stand at any particular time.

So how do you know this? You can't really count it like you would stock. But you can *measure* it. And you can *test* to see which elements are working and which are not. That's why I refer to this activity as *Testing and Measuring*. It's just another way of taking stock. But more on this later.

OK, so let's get practical.

Let's look at the *Average Dollar Sale Survey* first. Getting a handle on your Average Dollar Sale is not that difficult to do. In fact, it's very simple. Here's how:

- Design a simple survey form.

- Give it to each salesperson (or checkout person) and get her to fill it in each day for a limited period—let's say a week.

- Collate the forms and do the calculation.

This is what your Survey Form could look like:

AVERAGE DOLLAR SALE SURVEY

Date: _____

Salesperson: _____

CUSTOMER #   DOLLARS SPENT

_____   _____

_____   _____

_____   _____

_____   _____

_____   _____

_____   _____

_____   _____

_____   _____

_____   _____

DAILY SUMMARY

No. of Customers: _____

Total Dollars Spent: _____

Average Dollar Sale for the Day: _____
(Total Dollars ÷ No. of Customers)

Once you've completed this simple survey, you'll have an excellent idea of the Average Dollar Sale you're achieving at present. Now you'll know what you have to improve upon. You'll have a target—a benchmark against which to evaluate the strategies you'll soon be putting in place. All you have to do now is to decide what you've got to do to get there. And by Testing and Measuring after you've begun implementing your chosen strategies, you'll know when you've reached your objective, by how much you've improved, and the cost-effectiveness of the strategies. You'll also have a direct and accurate means of actually seeing the effect of these strategies on your bottom line.

Read through the powerful strategies outlined in this book, decide which you'd like to implement first, and then get into *Action*.

Let's now look at your *Margins Survey*.

Once again, it helps if you have a fair idea of what your margins are before you put in place strategies aimed at improving them. Some businesses will have different margins for different products, while others may work on a standard margin across the board. But whatever system you use, the important thing is to *know* what your margins are right now, before you start implementing strategies aimed at altering them.

Your form should look similar to the following figure:

MARGIN SURVEY

Date: _____

Department or Product Range	Item	Margin
_____	_____	_____
	_____	_____
	_____	_____
_____	_____	_____
	_____	_____
	_____	_____
_____	_____	_____
	_____	_____
	_____	_____
_____	_____	_____
	_____	_____
	_____	_____

Obviously the survey form you use should be designed to reflect the type of business you're in. Don't be afraid to alter it, redesign it, or create something entirely different. The important thing is to have a form you can use to help work out what your margins are.

Here's another thing that might surprise you: By just completing this simple exercise, you're already ahead of the pack. The vast majority of businesses really have no idea how they're performing on these two scores. And here's another surprise: You'll most probably find that just by putting the spotlight on these two areas, your business will improve.

But if you're after even more dramatic improvements, and who isn't, then read on. What I'm going to show you is easy to understand and implement. They have made a *huge* difference to literally thousands of businesses all over the world. Every day people contact me to tell me how much better they, and their businesses, are after having implemented these commonsense strategies.

One other thing: Spending time and effort finding out where you are at present will *save* you money in the long run. Once you know what your margins are, you'll be able to decide whether it's worth your while stocking low-margin items. It may very well be that they are worthwhile because of their high turnover rate, but at least you'll have the figures to justify your decision. It may also be that a high-margin item actually *costs* you money. It might not be worth the time, effort, and expense when all is taken into consideration. You see, as Quality Management guru Philip Crosby once said, eliminating what is not wanted or needed is profitable in itself.

Checking the current state of your business is like taking its temperature. It's vital for your business's, and your own, long-term well-being. Having an accurate picture of your Average Dollar Sales as well as your Margins is important for another reason; it helps shift attention away from turnover and onto profit. This is important because you can have the turnover you want, but unless you're making a profit, you're wasting your time. You'll go broke sooner or later.

So let's begin shifting that spotlight right now. Let's concentrate on profit. But before we begin thinking about what can be done to increase it, think for a moment about what the word actually means.

According to the dictionary, it is the return received on a business undertaking after all operating expenses have been met. Another explanation is the rate of increase in the net worth of a business enterprise in a given accounting period. It could also refer to the amount received for a commodity or service in excess of the original cost. These are obviously modern business definitions. But let's look at the root of the word for a moment. It comes from the Latin word *profectus*, or more particularly from the past participle of *proficere*, which means "to make progress or to profit." Let's break this word down further: *pro* means "forward," and facere means "to make." So the word "profit" actually means "to make progress forward." Isn't that interesting?

But let's progress this a little further, shall we? What does the present participle of the word *proficere* mean? It actually means "proficient." This is interesting, because when used as an adjective, proficient means "having or marked by an advanced degree of competence, as in an art, vocation, profession, or branch of learning." And when used as a noun, it means "an expert." Isn't that interesting?

Does this begin to throw new light on what profit is all about?

So it can be seen that if a business isn't profiting, it isn't going forward. Of course, going forward is the same thing as growing. I like to think of a business as being like a tree; if it isn't growing, it's dying. It simply can't do anything else. It certainly can't stand still and occupy some fictitious "middle ground." That's simply not possible. It either goes forward, or it goes backwards. It grows or it dies. It makes a profit or dies.

▌ Your Profit Chase Starts with You

We've all heard that time is our greatest asset. This is very true. You see, once you've spent your money, you can always earn more; but once you've spent your time, it's gone forever.

How you invest your time is one of the keys to business success. Understanding this, I'd like you to think about whether you have sufficiently assessed how you spend your time and how it could possibly be used more effectively? This is an important first step along the road to increased profit.

It's all about your attitude—and your outlook.

How serious are you about increasing the profit your business makes? Are you willing to do whatever it takes? Now don't jump to conclusions. I'm not suggesting you do the impossible or the outrageous. What I am suggesting is that you need to approach the quest for greater profitability from the right perspective. You need to start by examining *your* role in your business and what *you* can do to facilitate the chase.

Let me start by asking you this:

Do you know how to reduce the time you spend in your business while increasing your income at the same time?

Not possible? Committing financial suicide? Asking for trouble?

What if I suggested this is the first thing you need to do if you want your business to increase its level of profitability?

Let me explain.

You certainly can earn more while reducing the time you spend in your business, but only if you consider your time as an investment. Be aware that you need to invest your time rather than simply spend it. And understand that there is a rate of return on your time and that you need to ensure you're investing in techniques that will increase the profitability of your business.

So, invest your time in planning and setting goals to ensure the continuing growth of your business (and yourself).

To ensure this growth, business owners must calculate their productivity as a percentage of the total time spent in their business. Then they need to invest more time doing what will result in increased income, and less time on other demanding and unimportant tasks. Far too often I meet business owners who are spending time doing tasks in their business that should be left to a junior team member, or even a student, to do.

Why is this the case? Simple. You see, business owners, like everyone else, find it easier to spend time on things they know how to do—things they know they can do well—instead of on the things they know they *should* be doing, but don't really want to.

If you are guilty of this, then I want you to consider this question:

Is it better for you to focus 10 percent of your time on a task or have someone else give it 100 percent of their attention, even if that person is only half as good at it as you are?

After all, which is easier to achieve: a 100 percent improvement in your own productivity, or a 5 percent improvement in each of your employees' productivity? Think about it. You'll soon see what I'm getting at.

Are you in a position where you spend the majority of your time working *on* your business, by training, coaching, and nurturing your team members? Or are you uninterested in spending your valuable time safeguarding the long-term success of your business, *and* securing your freedom?

Understand this, to get your business to the stage where it provides you with the lifestyle you desire, you have to get paid what you are worth.

This means you'll need to prevent your time from being squandered on low priorities and develop a team that works without your being there. So, are you being paid what you are worth? Here's an interesting exercise that'll help you find out:

- Calculate the total hours that you work in your business each week (at your place of work as well as the time spent with work that you take home).

- Write down the amount that you pay yourself from your business each week and divide that amount by your total hours worked to arrive at your hourly rate.

- Now ask yourself this question: Is it actually legal to pay someone of your experience and qualification that hourly rate? Unfortunately for far too many people in business today, this exercise causes a high level of dissatisfaction.

Unless you make the effort to change what you are doing now and address issues such as these, you'll continue to get the results you've always gotten. Your business will continue to operate at the same level of profitability as it does now.

You need to change your approach to business if you want to drastically improve your bottom line.

OK, now that you have a new perspective on your role in your business, I want you to consider these points regarding your business in general:

- *Cost Reduction versus Income Growth.* So many business people focus all their attention on cost reduction—working long hours and cutting costs just to make ends meet. Now don't get me wrong, keeping your costs down is still one of the most important areas of business, but…

  If you really want to make money, you've got to generate more income. Making 10 times, or even 100 times, more profit than you do right now is more about increasing your income than it is about decreasing your costs.

  By the way, if you were to cut your costs by as much as you possibly can and still leave your company running, you'd probably only add about 10 or 20 percent to your bottom line. Yet through building your income, the bottom line jump is limitless.

- *Focus on Cashflow.* If you're not focused on creating cashflow, then you're wasting your time in business. Anyone can create a business that's no more than a job and make a living from it, but very few will ever create a massive cashflow gold mine. If that's what you're after, then you've got to understand that profit is the difference between cashflow in and cashflow out. Neither is more important than the other, but the in flow is where you get exponential growth.

- *Wallet Share versus Market Share.* Chasing market share in today's business world is a guaranteed formula for chasing your tail. Market share, or a focus on new customers, comes with the assumption that you're in the business of buying products or services and selling them to customers. If, however, you switch to the idea that you *buy* customers (because in reality you have to invest in marketing campaigns to attract them), you're no longer chasing market share; you're chasing wallet share. If you see it from this perspective, the issue now becomes one of how much, how many, and for how long can you sell to each customer you buy? In this world of business, where customer loyalty is everything, if you've already spent the money to buy a customer, then it makes total sense to make sure you get a full return on your investment. Chasing wallet share is as simple as remembering you've got a loyal customer base, so what else can you sell to them?

- *What Business Are You In?* Most business owners define their business by what they sell, like a fruit shop, an accounting service, and so on. Change from a product or service point of view to a marketing point of view and you'll realize you're actually in the *profit*-making business.

From now on you should think of marketing strictly as an investment, with customers as something that you buy, and start spending at least 50 percent of your time in this area of your business.

I've seen these simple concepts completely transform thousands of businesses that have been stuck on the treadmill of traditional thinking. It's time to get off the treadmill and start getting somewhere.

Remember, the transformation of your business's performance starts with you.

The 4 Ms of Profit

The funny thing is most people automatically think of the 4 Ps of Marketing when they think of the areas of business that management make decisions about: Product, Place, Price, and Promotion. Sure, they do have a say in these areas, but usually not directly. See, there are others (or there should be) who are more directly involved here. People like the Marketing Director, the Sales Manager, Financial Director, the Production Director, or the Distribution or Warehouse Manager. Of course, these positions can have different titles, and they could even be looked after by the same person, but for the sake of simplicity, let's assume they are handled by someone other than the business owner or manager.

Furthermore, marketing strategies, while they do ultimately have an influence on the profitability of a business (and sometimes a very negative one if a marketing campaign goes horribly wrong) usually take time to work their way through the system and onto the bottom line.

What this book is all about is what I call the 4 Ms of Profit. Marketing and all those related areas of business actually take place earlier on in the business schematic, the Business Chassis, whereas Profit is right at the end. If you are more interested in these earlier areas, then read my books *Instant Leads*, *Instant Promotions*, *Instant Sales*, and *Instant Repeat Business*. What I am talking about here is that last area of the Business Chassis—Profit.

OK, back to the 4 Ms of Profit. What are they? *Management* is the first of them. The others are *Money*, *Marketing*, and *Merchandise*. I must emphasize that I'm talking about those activities that take place at a higher level than the 4 Ps of Marketing. One other thing: the marketing referred to in the 4 Ms of Profit is not the same marketing as you'll find in the 4 Ps of Marketing.

Think of the difference between these two groups of concepts this way: The 4 Ps of Marketing are more operational, while the 4 Ms of Profit are more strategic. They cover the fundamental decisions only the business owner or manager can make.

And operating at the rear end of the Business Chassis, the results on the bottom line of profit-boosting strategies are very much more immediate or direct than those designed to affect earlier parts of the Business Chassis.

Implement a strategy aimed at generating more leads, and its results will affect only your bottom line very much later on, as they need time to filter through the system. However, implement a profit-boosting strategy and feel the effects almost immediately.

Understand this and you'll see why the marketing that belongs to the 4 Ps of Marketing is different than the marketing that falls under the 4 Ms of Profit. If this is confusing you, don't worry. It will become clear as you work your way through the book.

INSTANT PROFIT

$$\boxed{\textbf{Part 1}}$$

∎ Management

"OK, Charlie, so now we're going to discuss some of the various ways you can increase your profit. We're going to be looking at those specific strategies that have a direct bearing on profit. But you must understand that, while all the other strategies that we've already talked about, like ways to generate more leads, to better promote your business, to increase sales, and generate repeat business all do ultimately contribute to your bottom line, what I'm talking about now are those strategies that are more directly related to the concept of profit than to anything else."

I was keen to emphasize that everything one does in business will ultimately have an impact on profit, yet there are certain things that are more directly connected with the final outcome of one's business than others. You see, those elements of the Business Chassis that are nearer the front-end take time for their results to filter through towards the end—the profits.

"I'm with you, Brad. We'll be discussing things that, when implemented, will affect the amount of profit I make without having to do anything else. Is that right?"

"That's probably a good way of thinking of it, Charlie. Now because these profit-influencing strategies are many and varied, I'll group them into areas that roughly relate to the different key functions of any business—you know, those things that Management does that can directly influence profit, those that concern Sales and Marketing, those that are of a Financial nature, and those that have to do with Stock. This will allow you to easily relate them to your own situation."

"Yes, it will also make it easier to understand how they affect me directly. I guess it will also make it easier to decide which don't really affect me at all, if that's possible."

"You're catching on very fast, Charlie. Understanding how to run a business successfully isn't really all that difficult when you look at it in this way."

What Are Management-Related Strategies?

Before we begin considering what management-related strategies are, it might be beneficial to first consider what management is and what some leading lights have had to say about it.

According to the dictionary, management is defined as "the person or persons who control or direct a business or other enterprise." But by considering what some people have said about it we can gain a glimpse of this sometimes over-dramatized business concept.

According to Lee Iacocca, management is nothing more than motivating other people.

Peter F. Drucker says that management by objective works if you first think through your objectives. Ninety percent of the time you haven't. Isn't that interesting?

Surround yourself with the best people you can find, delegate authority, and don't interfere, says Ronald Reagan.

And John W. Teets says that management's job is to see the company not as it is, but as it can become.

All of these shed an interesting perspective on the topic of management. What is clear is that it is an all-encompassing area that covers a vast territory on the business landscape. So how does this relate to strategies aimed at having a dramatic influence on the profitability of a company? And what are these strategies?

When focusing on strategies that will, in one way or another, directly influence the profit a business makes, the ones that spring to mind first are those that are generally believed to be the preserve of the manager. After all, isn't that what management does—look after the profit side of the business?

What then, are these "management things" that have a direct relationship with the profit a business makes? In general terms, they are the decisions management makes that it wouldn't generally expect others to become involved with. And they are things the business owner could implement almost immediately. They are the types of decisions only management would make that are designed to have a very rapid and direct influence on the company's profitability.

The Strategies

Provide Team Training

By ensuring your team is multiskilled, you can cut down on costs. You won't have to hire a temp when one of your team members takes leave or is off sick. Other team members will easily be able to cover for them.

Not only does this save you money, but it also provides your team with variety. They will then appreciate more fully the magnitude of the business and begin to feel more useful. This, in turn, will have flow-on effects as far as productivity and morale are concerned.

Team training really is one of the best investments you can make. Give people real responsibility and they will rise to the challenge. They'll view it as an investment in their own futures. But don't expect them to do something they feel ill-equipped to do.

Team training is also an excellent way of building team spirit. Make sure it's fun too.

Let me give you a great example:

One of my Coaches, Graham Dunkley, was working with a Harvey Norman store in Maitland, New South Wales, recently. This store was the smallest retail outlet in the Group and was underperforming. Glen Gregory, the store's owner, was very ambitious and wanted to do better.

Graham promised that he would be able to achieve greater results, but it was ultimately up to him. Graham would give him the tools to grow the business, but he would have to put in the hard work.

Graham then talked him into putting his entire team through a one-day sales course. Needless to say this included Glen too! The team members suddenly realized they could do other things besides discounting!

They came back all fired up.

Glen then had his Coach put them through team training, and once again he included himself in that team. He suddenly realized that anyone can manage, but it takes skill to be a leader and to communicate well.

He began learning all about leverage in business.

Glen and his team were taught that all the national advertising in the world only gets the prospect to the door. What the team does from that moment on, to make it a memorable buying experience, is what explodes a business and takes them all to the top.

They learned that treating their clients with honor, respect, warmth, and empathy creates a long-term, trusting relationship, which then spawns greater opportunities for profitable sales than all the incessant giveaways that are traditionally featured in TV advertising.

Suddenly their conversion rate, transaction rate, and profitability climbed, and best of all, this "new" team started having fun!

Within a short period of time, Glen's store had become the Group's number-three performer!

Another great benefit you'll receive from training your team members is that they'll begin working like a real team. What do I mean by this? Let me explain by changing tack for a while.

All too often the cry is heard, "you can't get good people," or "why can't I get my people to do as I tell them?" Well, life could be a lot easier for business owners if only they would train their teams.

Consider, for a moment, the business owner who, despite having 10 people working in the business, ends up doing all the work. Sound familiar? If it is, then what's the point of being in business?

First, get back to basics. Most people in business will understand how important systems are. Systems usually allow a business to run smoothly (and profitably). With systems in place, it's simply a matter of employing people to run those systems. A good example of this is, of course, McDonalds. With a food product that, at best, could only be described as average, it is their systems that keep it a hugely successful entity.

Implementing systems and then getting your people to work as a team are the basic foundations of any business. Understand this: the result of these two equals more than the sum of the parts.

So, the systems have been built and are clearly defined, and now it's a matter of having the right people to run those systems. However, the real challenge lies ahead. It's not just a matter of having people who come in follow the system and get the job done. What you are looking for now is *synergy*.

Synergy comes from having people who are committed to a common goal. If people are involved in setting the common goal, they are generally more likely to commit to it. If you, as the business owner, dictate to your team members what the goal is, don't expect much commitment from them. If your team members have ownership, they are much more likely to achieve.

Finally, be aware of what you are teaching your team. Think of it this way: if a baby cries and its mother comes running, what will the baby learn to do after a while? Exactly. Let out a cry and in rushes mom. All I ask is for you to be very aware of what you are teaching your team. If your attitude is that no one can do the job as well as you can and you jump in and do it, your team will learn from that.

Putting together the dream team for your business can be as easy as taking an action approach rather than an information approach. With the plethora of training options available to employers, it can often be puzzling to find the strategies that are going to achieve results.

There is one basic rule to apply when considering your next team-building exercise. Dream teams are not built through information or training alone. Seminars, competency training, reading books, and watching videos are all helpful strategies, but as the age old adage goes, action speaks louder than words. Being able to perform tasks during training is not the same as applying them on a day-to-day basis. And remember, information alone does not automatically change behavior. For example, we read about the dangers of smoking but many people still smoke.

Environment is one of the key factors in influencing your team's success rate. People base their behavior on their beliefs about themselves and their environment. Can they have a positive impact on their environment? Does this environment support positive behavior? Team members should feel that they have the capability to contribute in their current environment. This means that giving them the right equipment and environment to be effective is essential. It also helps if they feel safe to contribute, if they have a supportive environment.

But how do you find this out? You simply have to ask. Ask your team if they think there are factors in their environment that could be improved to help them be more efficient, productive, or happy. Perhaps they may prefer music while they work. Or better lighting or more flexible hours. Many organizations have realized the importance of employee satisfaction to the bottom line. Progressive workplaces now include childcare facilities and ergonomically designed workstations.

Beliefs are the key motivators in people's behavior patterns. However, changing your team members' beliefs is not an easy or swift task. Recruiting the right people through personality instruments and team interviews can be one strategy, and understanding their beliefs can be important in identifying others.

Common beliefs limiting team performance include:

- Feedback. "I have some constructive feedback but expressing it may cause a confrontation—best to keep it to myself."

- Delegation. "The only way to get the job done properly is to do it myself."

- Sales. "Real salespeople are dishonest, pushy, and arrogant."

Changing beliefs such as these can be a daunting challenge. Team leaders need to facilitate change by designing flexible experiences for people in organizations to learn that "maybe there is a different way to look at this." Experiential learning such as climbing trees and playing games are used because they are fun, help build relationships, and because they work. Multiple and varied experiences must be used to inspire new ways of seeing and thinking about things. Reframing opens the mind to new beliefs and patterns of behavior.

Information and ideas alone are not enough. They need to be ingrained in day-to-day activity. You need to look at training options and ask what beliefs in your organization may hamper or aid the achievement of your desired outcomes. How can your work environment be changed to support flexibility and greater productivity, and what experiences will help foster changes in belief and behaviors?

Remember that team building is not an exact science but a tool for finding the best strategies available to bring out the very best in your team.

Another thing you need to do is to train your team to make use of scripts. This is a very popular strategy that really does impact on your bottom line. You see, scripts give your team members consistency when dealing with sales enquiries and objections. They are developed based on what is known to work for successful members of your team.

Just think about this: In your team you're bound to have one or two people who perform way better than the others when it comes to sales. (I'm using sales here as an example—the same would apply to other areas of your business where your team members need to interact with customers with a view to bringing in business.) Why is this? Is it simply because they have the gift of the gab? Or is it because they are more experienced or just better salespeople? Either way, it doesn't matter. What does is that your team learns from what they are doing. If they were to emulate your best salesperson, to copy what that person does, then chances are they too will achieve similar results. The best way to ensure this is for them to use scripts. A script is just like a recipe. If you want to bake a cake just like the one your grandma used to make, follow her recipe and you'll end up with a similar cake. It's no different with business. If you want your salespeople to emulate your most successful salesperson, give them a script to follow. That way all the important points are raised, all the "hot buttons" are pushed, and a sequence is followed that leads to a logical conclusion. But before we discuss what a script should include, you need to consider these four main points when planning one:

- *Targeted Lists*: You don't want to speak to anyone who would not be interested in your product or service.

- *Process*: You need to plan your process. It's unlikely you'll sell large, expensive items in one step, and you're really kidding yourself if you can't close a $50 sale in two steps or less.

- *Urgency*: People can put off buying forever. If you don't give them a reason to act now, your script will be unlikely to work.

- *You-Focus*: Your script needs to be focused on the customer. If it says "I" and "we" throughout, it's likely to bore them, and you can't bore anyone into buying from you.

You need to say something like this: "So it sounds like *you* need this. By buying from us, *you* will get that plus a whole lot more, and I know that's important to *you*."

In short, a successful script is based on a successful idea. It doesn't matter which way you say something that's uninteresting, unappealing, and unaffordable. It'll still sound like rubbish. Likewise, if you've got a great offer and product, and you've really targeted the market well, there's not much you can do to go wrong.

Give some thought to the overall picture first. Is what you're offering really worth the trouble of marketing it? Perhaps you might have to face the hard reality that the reason your business is not succeeding is simple—it's a bad business.

Remember, if your business seems impossible to market, perhaps it is. But by the same token, you'll never know until you try.

OK, you should now be in a position to begin writing a powerful script that is tailor-made for your own situation. Here's how to go about it:

Step 1

Identify exactly who the people of your target market are. You must know their average age, their sex, their level of income, where they live, and what level of education they have.

Step 2

Decide where you are going to find a suitable list of prospects. You could source them from a database (it could be bought from a broker, from another business, or you could create your own), from a contest you could run, or you could simply look through the telephone book. Of course, your prospects could also simply walk in through the door of your store.

Step 3

Decide what you want to say to your prospects. Your script needs to have a clear purpose; it needs to take people from Point A to Point B. What are those points? Point A is your initial statement. The rest of the script should lead to Point B, which is where you ask the prospect to act now—to commit.

It's most important to understand your customers. If you understand their needs, their wants, and their position, you can sell almost anything to them. But before writing anything, you need to decide exactly what you want your prospects to do on hearing your script. What is your Point B? Do you want them to use a credit card then and there, or do you want them to simply make an appointment?

Of course, there's a different psychology behind each type of objective. To make a sale, you need to answer all their objections. To make an appointment, you simply have to suggest that any objections they have can be answered, and will be addressed in detail further down the track.

Once you know what you want to achieve, you need to put yourself in their position. What do they already know about you? This is your Point A. How do they feel about you? How do they generally feel about your product or service? How often have people in your industry harassed them? Do they want to spend a lot of time or just get it over with? What objections do they have? What else is important?

Now, you have to determine the path from Point A to Point B. How can you lead people through the decision-making process?

We'll work that out next, but first, let's deal with something even more important.

It pays to remember that simply asking people to act now (or for that matter, *telling* them to act now) is rarely enough. You need to give them a good reason why *now* is the time to do something.

See, most purchases can be delayed forever. It's one thing to create desire, but it's another to actually get people to part with their cash. Every month, customers have to decide what to spend their money on. After all, they all have different priorities.

The question now becomes, how do you offer a great deal without slicing your profit margin drastically? Here are a couple of ways to think about. They will be discussed in more detail later on in this book, but for now they'll give you an idea of what can be done to help the decision-making process along. Adapt these ideas to suit your situation. Come back to this after you've read this book and reread this section.

First, make sure you are selling products or services that have a high margin. Often, that's not possible—try getting a high margin on gasoline. If you have the option of gearing your business toward higher margin items, do so, as it'll make it much easier for you to come up with great deals later on.

If you can't do this, you need to find items or services that are highly valued by the customer, yet have a low cost to you. Extra service is an old standby here. Information booklets are another. Even better are services you can get for free from other businesses. For example, a hairdresser could offer to introduce her clients to a beauty salon, if the beauty salon agrees to give every customer a free facial.

Of course, you can create urgency by placing a limitation on the availability of your offer. You could say these prices will be available only for the next two weeks until the new model arrives, or that prices are about to rise, or that you'll only be in town for the next four days. Naturally, being truthful is better—people are excellent at picking up on insincerity.

Step 4

Decide how you are going to write your script. A lot will depend on the type of script you need. For instance, it could be used for telemarketing (either cold-calling or as a follow-up on direct mail), door-to-door sales, answering an incoming telephone enquiry, or for in-store enquiries from customers. They will vary slightly depending on the situation, but they will basically include a greeting, a reason for the call, some open-ended questions, getting agreement, dealing with objections, and a close.

For more details about how to write scripts, read my book *Instant Sales*.

Concentrate on "A"-Grade Customers Only. Sack "C"- and "D"-Grade Customers

Now, I know many of you will find this a strange thing to do, but get rid of your "C"- and "D"-Grade customers—you don't need them.

What are "C"- and "D"-Grade customers? They are the ones that basically waste your time. They are constantly on the lookout for bargains, discounts, or rejects. They are what the automobile trade calls "tire kickers."

Let them know you don't want to deal with them; but don't be rude or offensive about it. Drop subtle hints. Write to them or give them a handout that clarifies your rules. Spell out what you expect of them, what the standards of your business are, and what your business and customer policies are.

Take the case of a pub in Tasmania. It was a great watering hole and a very successful business. However, as the area became more popular with tourists, the owner noticed his clientele was slowly changing. Whereas previously the pub attracted local businessmen, politicians, and the more intellectual type of people, it had become more popular with backpackers, bikers, and the younger set.

Now, there might be nothing wrong with this newer type of customer, but the owner (and the regulars) didn't like it. So, for the sake of his regulars and his reputation, he decided to "sack" these new customers.

How did he do this? Simple. He changed the type of music played in the pub. No more pop or modern music. From that moment on it was strictly classical music only. The younger element disappeared almost overnight, and without any trouble at all.

Here's another great example. One of my New Zealand Business Coaches, Steve McDonald, was working with a computer software company called Achieve! Ltd. Its owner, Mary Sue Severn, was having all sorts of challenges, one of which happened to be a difficult customer. This is what she says:

"Here's another thing Steve helped me with: I actually 'resigned' a customer! I sacked this customer I didn't want to work with any more. And it was so hard! Man. I thought, 'I owe it to them,' and he said, 'but you don't deserve to be treated that way.' And he actually let me get over that hurdle of, 'my gosh, I can actually get rid of a client who doesn't respect me and who doesn't treat me well.' In the end I'm so glad I did, because the client got into all kinds of trouble and is now out of business. I'm so glad that I wasn't part of all that trouble he had after I resigned him. And I think that he was probably shocked receiving that letter from me—hearing that I didn't want to work with him any more.

"Steve actually held my hand (not literally) through this whole process. I mean, I was shaking as I typed the letter, and shaking as I put it into the envelope, but you know, he just said, 'You just have to do it. Do it.' And I just closed my eyes and put blind faith in what he said. In the end it was very right to do it.

"And now, I could do it again if I have to. He taught me that if you can do it once, you could do it again. He often says you get the customers you deserve. And that's one thing that I've found really valuable to keep in my mind. When I look back at the customers I have now, I just appreciate them all so much because I think I've started to attract, or draw, those people that I want to have as customers, instead of just having a customer for the sake of having one. So, by Steve's saying, 'You get the customers you deserve,' it has become a self-fulfilling prophecy."

Of course, you do need to think carefully about this strategy, because it may be that "C"- and "D"-Grade customers are your bread and butter. It might be that if you were to sack them, you'd have no business to speak of. Or you might then have to relaunch or reposition your business with a whole new target market in mind. Now that may not be such a bad thing, but it all depends on your individual situation.

Bear in mind the 80-20 rule that applies to most businesses. Eighty percent of your profit comes from 20 percent of your customers. These are your "A"-Grade customers. Why then should you put up with so much, and spend so much time and effort appeasing 80 percent of your clients if they don't contribute much to your bottom line? Concentrate on those who do.

Keep an Accurate Database

By regularly updating your database, you'll be sure your time and money are being well spent. Nobody wants to waste time and money trying to contact people when they have outdated information on them. What's more, they could be inactive customers—people no longer interested in what you have to offer.

Take real estate sales, for instance. If you were a real estate salesperson, you'd be keeping contact details of everyone who makes contact with you, be that from open for inspections, office walk-ins, or as a result of newspaper or window advertisements. And you'd be maintaining a good record-keeping system that would indicate when they made contact, what was discussed, what their needs were, what the budget is, and which properties you've shown them. You'd also keep records of what they thought of each property and how much they would be prepared to pay for each. You see, not only will this information help you to accurately match their requirements with those properties you have on your books, but you'd also be able to provide your sellers with real market feedback.

Now, if you were to make contact with 10 or 20 prospective buyers each day, in a month you'd have amassed a sizable, and potentially valuable, database of well-qualified prosects. But unless you diligently updated it, you'd quickly end up with a wad of useless information. You see, what happens is that, as the days go by, many actually buy properties from other real estate agents. As soon as this happens, they're no longer on the market. And they probably wouldn't reenter the market for another six or seven years.

So unless you regularly update your database through keeping in contact with the people on it, you'd waste a lot of time that could be more productively and lucratively spent chasing other listings or buyers. Money saved here goes directly to your bottom line.

Purchase Authorization

Only allow your team members to make purchases with an authorized Purchase Order. Yes, I know this may sound draconian, but controlling your outgoings is one of the surest, simplest ways to make sure there is no unnecessary financial profit drain.

Remember the old saying, look after the pennies and the pounds will look after themselves? It's quite true. Over the years I've come across hundreds of companies that allow all sorts of people to place orders for whatever they need. The idea's great, but think about the wastage. See, if every department or section looks after its own ordering, there's inevitably going to be massive duplication resulting in too much stock on hand.

And it's not just in controlling the ordering of major stock items that will add to your profitability; it's also by controlling the reordering of small, everyday office supplies like photocopy paper, pens, printer cartridges as well as calculators, computers, and kitchen supplies that will make a noticeable difference. You see, by taking steps to coordinate and control this function, you'll also be able to maximize your bulk-buying power and save even more. And of course, savings here means more profit.

By instituting a system whereby an authorized Purchase Order is necessary before anything can be bought, you'll be ensuring that your money is being well spent, that the best prices are being paid because they'll be ordered against a prearranged bulk purchasing arrangement with a particular supplier, and that only what's absolutely necessary will be bought.

You must let your team members know that these measures are being instituted, not because you don't trust them, but because it's crucial for proper planning and prudent accounting. It'll also make people stop to think if what they want is absolutely necessary.

Take, for example, a company that is structured along departmental lines. Let's assume there are four departments: sales, finance, manufacturing and administration. Suppose, too, that each department does its own ordering and independently orders a box of ballpoint pens because a person in each department suddenly needs one. The company would end up with four boxes of ballpoint pens. If there are 25 pens in each box, they have collectively bought 100, and all because they need just four. Better to coordinate their purchasing arrangements and buy one box. That way they'd still end up with 21 in stock after handing one each to those who require one. And they'd most probably have bought them far cheaper, because the Administrative Manager would have done a deal with the supplier to cover all their administrative supplies for the year. They would have enjoyed a bulk discount.

Now this may be an oversimplification, but it illustrates the point I'm making. Take care of the details, and you'll see the results reflected on your bottom line.

Remuneration

This has got to be one of the most emotional subjects in business. It is for this, after all, that the vast majority of people seek employment. Sure, everyone would like to earn as much as possible, while business owners would love to pay as little as possible, but the trick is to strike a happy medium. It's no use paying rock-bottom wages because then you'll attract the type of team member that is willing to work for little. You get what you pay for. Or as my Dad once said, you get the team members you deserve.

Now it may very well be that your business is perfectly suited to the cheapest type of labor available. If so, that's fine. But generally speaking, you need to ensure your wages are, at the very least, competitive or market related.

An important aspect to your total remuneration bill is the amount of money you spend on overtime pay. It's important to bear in mind that every time you pay team members for overtime worked, you're eating into your profits. Cut overtime payments and you'll see an immediate improvement to your bottom line.

How do you do this without inviting a backlash if you currently pay overtime? The best way is, of course, to let new team members know you don't pay overtime at the time they are being interviewed for the job. That way the problem doesn't arise.

But what if you already have team members who are used to being paid for the overtime they put in? This is a little trickier. What you could do is to negotiate a flextime arrangement whereby they get time off in lieu of overtime pay. That way they'll be saving on the tax they pay.

Another approach is to replan the daily schedules or procedures so that all work is taken care of during normal business hours. This may mean you might have to have a closer look at your systems. It might also mean you might have to put new systems in place to ensure everything gets done during normal working hours.

You could offer team members various other perks as a trade-off for not receiving overtime payment—things like product or services that your business might specialize in. Products from other businesses could be sourced as part of an intercompany strategic alliance.

But why should you, the business owner, be the only one concerned with margins and profits? Your team members can assist you in boosting your margins, particularly if you make it worth their while. So, offer them an incentive based on margins. What about paying your sales team a higher commission on anything they sell at the full price? This will allow you to fix your margins, not just your commission percentages.

If you decide to use this approach, make sure all your team members have a clear understanding of what the margins are. Spell out the numbers. They need to know at what level their commission stops. And don't forget to offer them a larger reward for sales made at full margin.

Now, here's another thing to consider. Many directors draw far too much money from their companies, and this often leads to cashflow problems. Be sensible about how much you pay yourself. You see, it's really important to have a pool of cash available in the business so you can meet unexpected costs as they arise, and also so you can take advantage of investment opportunities as they crop up.

In any event, you can always draw director's fees as profits at the end of the financial year when you know you can afford to. Also consider reinvesting these fees in the business, as there are tax advantages if you do.

Efficiency, Productivity, and Time Management

It may seem rather obvious to you, but you'll be surprised at how many companies waste large sums of money in these three areas. Make improvements here and you'll notice an immediate improvement on your bottom line.

Start by evaluating each of these areas separately. Look at each team member's job description and make sure you clearly spell out what's expected of him in each of these areas. Then institute a performance-based reward system.

By reviewing these job descriptions and then analyzing and evaluating what each team member actually does, you'll quickly identify which areas are costing you money. Fix them by letting your team members know what the minimum performance standards are.

You'll find that just by focusing on efficiency, productivity, and time management, your team's performance will improve. This is because your team members will become more aware of what they do, how they do it, and how they could do it better. They'll quickly become conscious that their performances are being monitored. It'll keep them on their toes.

Some companies are quite innovative in the way they go about encouraging improvements in productivity. Some have in place a system whereby team members can borrow company equipment over the weekends, because they know this often leads to better and more efficient ways of operating. They are quite happy to encourage better performance levels through assisting their people in overcoming personal challenges at home, by letting them take home laptop computers or digital cameras, for instance.

Once you've tightened up on the efficiency and productivity of each team member through better time management or improved systems, you may well be able to gain further improvements to your bottom line by reducing the size of your team accordingly. You see, by carefully refining your systems, you will probably be able to cut down on the idle time most team members have during the working day.

By running a tighter business, you'll also be able to consolidate various team functions without negatively affecting productivity. And by being able to eliminate just one position in this way, you'll make a major cost saving, which will have an immediate impact on your bottom line.

Bear in mind that the wages of even the most junior team member amount to a sizeable expense for any business.

Because this is a very delicate area to be concentrating on when trying to minimize expenditure, you'll need to proceed with care and tact. Here are some suggestions that might be of use:

- Closely analyze the output of each individual. The mere fact that they are being monitored will result in an increase in productivity, which means idle time will be kept to a minimum.

- Give team members more work and see if they cope. You'll be surprised at how much people can handle. By taking on more little by little, the total amount of work that needs to be done might be spread among fewer people.

- Embrace new technology that is making the workplace more efficient.

- Let natural attrition take care of reducing the size of your team. When employees leave, don't replace them. And if you have forewarning that someone is going to be leaving in the not-too-distant future (such as when someone is coming up for retirement), take advantage of the situation and reorganize or resystematize to compact and consolidate your team.

Of course, it's not just among the ranks of your workers that savings can be made. You must also turn your attention to your management.

One of the problems with many modern businesses is that they are top heavy—they have too many levels of management. By putting systems in place and improving the training of your team, it may be possible to make some of your management positions redundant.

So how do you go about this? Here's a suggestion:

- Develop a culture of delegating. Let those operating at lower levels have more authority. Give them responsibility—real responsibility. If people are actually doing the work, why shouldn't they be accountable for it as well? Let them take operational decisions regarding their areas of expertise.

- Design and implement systems that allow team members to work unsupervised. Start by looking at the most basic things like answering the phone all the way through to how you manufacture your product. Design them so they're clearly defined and easy to understand; that way your employees will know what you expect of them. Preferably write them down and turn them into checklists.

- Be sure to reward those who work unsupervised for meeting their goals. This is usually a lot cheaper than paying a manager to supervise them.

By focusing on improving efficiency, productivity, and time management, one of the benefits will be a drastic reduction of duplication in your business. This will lead to an impressive improvement in your profit situation because double handling and unnecessary paperwork cost most companies many thousands of dollars each year. It not only costs, but it's needless, wasteful, and, quite frankly, it's insanity.

Encourage your team members to complain about duplication or wasted time spent on paperwork. And remember constantly to audit your systems, as it's so easy to allow improvements made in this area to lapse. It might be necessary to relieve your sales team of their administrative burden. Let them get on with the job of selling. Get someone else to attend to the paperwork. It'll be well worth it in the long run.

While talking about duplication, there's more to it than at first meets the eye. You see, making sure you do things right the first time will pay huge dividends as far as improving your efficiency and productivity is concerned. Think about how much time you or your team is wasting by having to do the same thing more than once. That's money straight down the drain. You see, you only get paid once to do most things, so if you don't do it right the first time, your profits can quickly dwindle. For example, mechanics that charge by the hour will waste much of their profit on a job if they have to redo it. So, taking a bit longer and doing it right the first time can be well worthwhile.

This is where training comes in. Invest in good training programs so that your employees have the opportunity to become experts at doing their jobs fast and right the first time. And don't skimp on quality, because having to repair something costs you much more in the long run. Many automobile manufacturers have actually gone to the wall through sloppy workmanship that resulted in an avalanche of warranty claims that they couldn't afford. And sure, make mistakes—but only once.

Let me give you another great example of this. Remember DK Design Kitchens? Well, the company was getting nowhere fast. It was having problems with the team, who wasn't enjoying coming to work anymore. The team also spending a lot of time "reworking orders" because of sloppy workmanship.

Things quickly came to a head and the owners couldn't take it anymore. Coach Greg Albert was called in.

When he arrived, the situation was that the business was running; yet the major items like culture, the team, or going the extra mile were just not happening. So this is where he spent most of his early time there, basically getting the owners to become real leaders by inspiring people to follow, rather than just telling them what to do!

He spent time developing all the *spiritual* points of the business first—the Culture, Vision, Mission, Rules, etc. He then relaunched the company to the team.

Once this had taken place, he worked on the development of the sales team and its marketing activities. Testing and Measuring had become a culture, embedded into the way things were done. The company tried different techniques and methods until it found something that worked.

Once this was all working efficiently, the company put Key Performance Indicators (KPIs) and management tools in place, and spent a long time on the financial management side of the business. Soon they had spreadsheets and graphs for everything from Cashflow and Sales, and from Conversion to Factory Efficiency. This really gave them a sense of understanding and control of the business.

The company's biggest achievement was working out its new price list, changing the commission structure, and changing the manner in which it quoted for new business. Greg really made the company focus on profit, not turnover. As a result, it suddenly began making more profit with a lot less effort.

During the next 12 months, the average dollar sale increased by 40 percent and it increased prices by 10 percent. This resulted in an increase in turnover of 30 percent, but more significantly its profitability became much healthier. Whereas the business previously ran at a slight loss, they turned this around to recording a net profit of $250,000 on a turnover of $3 million.

Accounts, Cashflow, and Profit and Loss are now reviewed monthly. And everyone knows their targets. Of course, the company still faces challenges, which it tries to solve as they arise. The difference now is that all challenges are analyzed and understood so they don't occur again. And for the first time the owners feel in control.

Becoming more efficient means making maximum use of your time, and this increases your productivity. The same, of course, applies to your business as a whole. So once you've increased your efficiency, chances are you've got some idle time or spare capacity on your hands. Now if you run a service-based business, then this is definitely an area that you need to look at.

For businesspeople such as plumbers, mechanics, or accountants, who make their money from charging an hourly rate, promoting idle time is critical. So to get clients coming in during quiet periods, you should look at offering a reduced rate or additional free service. Remember that operating at a slightly reduced fee during these periods of idle time is better than not operating at all. Restaurants can even get their past customers back on slower nights with a "Tuesday Night Club."

There's a variation to this theme, and that's to rent out idle space. You see, having all your space working for you has got to be more efficient and profitable than having half your warehouse, office, or factory being unused. Rent it out. In many cases it'll be worth your while renovating the area just to make it more attractive as a rental proposition. The extra revenue it will provide will be straight profit. Furthermore, there could be further benefits, particularly if you were to rent it out to a company that complements yours. For example, if you ran an automobile repair shop, you could gain synergy by renting out some idle space to a car detailer, tire company, or muffler supplier. The opportunities are endless. All you need to do is to apply some lateral thinking and you could soon be seeing a much healthier bottom line.

Systematize the Routine and Humanize the Exceptions

Put systems in place to cut down on your team's workload. Effective systems can often allow people who are performing those tasks to perform them at a higher level or to perform more tasks in the same amount of time.

So how do you go about doing this if you don't have any systems in place at present?

Start off by making a list of all the routine tasks that each team member is responsible for each day. Then write or record on video or audiotape exactly what needs to be done, how it must be done, what happens if it the task can't be carried out as specified, who needs to be notified and when, what follow-up action is required, and what, if any, administrative work needs to be carried out. This could be written down in the form of a flowchart. It needs to be done for each and every task that each and every team member is responsible for. Then collate these into functional areas like sales, merchandising, manufacturing, or front office. Collectively they form a system.

Think of it this way: a system is just a documented, methodical, learnable, effective way of ensuring individual tasks get done effectively and efficiently. It is a written process on paper, designed to give the responsible team member control of the task and to create a desired result.

There are many ways to write systems. Here's an example of how to go about writing one for salespeople: Ask your number-one salesperson to write down the answer to the question, "Exactly what do you say to prospects to get them to buy your product?" You may even choose to reward your top salesperson for doing this by offering a great incentive such as a percentage of extra sales.

Once you have systems in place, regularly audit all the tasks and ask, "Could this be done better using a different system?" Remember the customer—there are some things that a machine just can't do.

Let me give you a real-life example as an illustration.

If you were to walk down Cuba Street in Wellington, New Zealand, you'll come across Café Istanbul. Now, the restaurant business has its own unique set of challenges like unsocial working hours, long working nights (and days), and a high turnover of staff. Behind the scenes in the kitchen there are challenges too concerning stocking levels, choice of menus, preparation time, and the minimization of wastage. The result is that restaurant owners don't lead a normal life, resulting all too often in their eventually selling or burning out.

Fortunately for the owners of Café Istanbul, they decided to take action to ensure this didn't happen to them. And it so easily could have. You see, their business was stable but unspectacular. Sales were declining, and there were continual challenges recruiting and retaining a competent team. They were getting good numbers of diners on Thursdays, Fridays, and Saturdays, but for the remainder of the week they were operating marginally at best, or at a slight loss.

They faced several challenges before they met Coach Steve McDonald. These included staffing in the kitchen (they used to import chefs from Turkey), team building with their front-of-house team, and getting the right people. Other challenges included putting systems in place that, perhaps, they hadn't thought of before.

Steve got them to think about systematizing the routine and humanizing the exceptions. Now they've got a really good booking management system, and they've diverted the phone so they take all of the bookings, which they now manage better. Before it was left up to the kitchen staff, many of whom could hardly speak English. It was a case of when the restaurant was full it was full.

Steve also introduced a system to use at night to allocate tables and direct people to them. They now know who's going where and how long they'll need at their table. So it's little things like this that make the whole running of the restaurant a lot smoother.

Since coaching began, sales increased by 20 percent and customer numbers and the average dollar sales are consistently up on a weekly basis.

The team members are now more stable and more productive. They have a greater focus on creating an exceptional dining experience for every customer, every time.

The owners now work four or five days per week only, and have time off together every week. They now have a life. And they are well on the way to having a manager who can run the business without them, for longer periods. The team is also far more productive, happier, and stable.

The kitchen is now essentially a self-sustaining, self-contained unit. Orders, cleaning, and kitchen activities are self-managed by the kitchen team—the owners don't need to continually supervise that area any longer.

Tasks such as ordering and maintenance, as well as daily team management and operations, are at a point where the systems run the business. The owners are now able to work *on* their business rather than *in* it.

What Else?

Of course, there's much more you can still do to improve the profitability of your business. Thankfully, it's simply not possible to produce a finite list—the possibilities are endless and are limited only by your imagination and entrepreneurial spirit.

But here are some more to consider:

- Improve your negotiating skills. You need to be strong in this area if you want to get the best deals. Everything from employment agreements to getting the best deals from your suppliers depends on your skill in this field. Rehearsing in front of a mirror or practicing in the car as you drive can develop these skills. You need to make sure you're getting the best deals from your suppliers so that you're making the maximum profit from selling their products.

- Recycle wherever possible. There are many different products you can recycle to help reduce expenses. If you have a photocopier, then use both sides of the paper, or buy refillable ink cartridges for your printer. By taking the time to recycle, it's possible to save a considerable amount of money over a period of time. And this savings will show up on your bottom line.

- Work two or even three shifts. This is a great idea for any business looking to cut down on the amount of equipment it needs to purchase. For example, a data entry company could run two shifts rather than buying two sets of computers. This eliminates the need to pay overtime as well as saving money on equipment.

- Consider running your business from smaller premises. Redesign your operation so you can run it with much smaller outlets. If you have excess floor space, then you have one of two options: you can either rent the unused space to another business or move to smaller premises. If you're paying for floor space that's not being used (or not likely to be used anytime soon), then move *now*!

- Work from home. Many people believe that when they go into business for themselves they must rent an office or storefront. The truth is that many small businesses can be run from home. This cuts down on your overhead and transportation costs, as you don't need to commute to work. You also have the added advantage of paying only one lot of bills and receiving a number of tax benefits. So if working from home is an option, then you should take advantage of it, because lower overhead means greater profits. Or, go one step further and let your team work from home.

- Run your business as a mobile business. This can be a great one for mechanics and hairdressers in particular. As with working from home, having a mobile business dramatically reduces your overhead. And having reduced overhead means less to come out of your income. This, in anyone's language, means more profit. Running a mobile business also offers attractive tax benefits to you, and convenience benefits to your customers.

- Invest in technology. This will improve the speed at which your business operates. You need to have the fastest, most reliable machines that you can afford. You should also have all your accounts and files on computer. To do any bookkeeping manually in this day and age is criminal. So set a budget and buy the best you can afford. Don't worry too much about technology's becoming obsolete, as you'll eventually have to dive in and buy, so why wait? And if you're looking at upgrading your accounting package, look for one that's compatible with that used by your accountant. This will enable you to work together electronically. It's more efficient and will save you heaps of time.

- Employ people in-house. This is a great way for you to reduce your expenses and increase your margins. In many cases it's far less expensive to pay somebody a wage than it is to subcontract the work out. A good example would be a business that regularly uses the services of a graphic designer. If the hourly rate for subcontract work was $70, but the designer could be employed to work full time for $24 per hour, then employing in-house would make more sense.

- Outsource when necessary. It is not always less expensive to employ someone in-house. If you don't have enough work to keep that employee busy full time, or if the cost of the equipment the employee needs is too great, you're better off outsourcing the work.

- Move premises if you need to ship your goods over a long distance. You see, moving could then save you the cost of transportation. Another reason to consider moving would be to save money on rent. Not all areas command the same rents, so look for a cheaper option. This is a good idea for any business that doesn't rely on passing traffic.

- Stop running ads that don't work. This sounds obvious, but you'd be surprised how many business owners persist with ads that just don't do anything for them. If your ads aren't making you money, then stop running them. You should run only ads that make you money immediately. It is important to test and measure each one to make sure that you're getting the maximum return possible. But when you find one that works, keep using it.

- Check your bills. Again, this may sound obvious, but when you're chasing profit, you need to tighten up every area of your business. You see, every little thing helps. Don't assume that your bills are correct. In many cases you may find you've been overcharged, and in others you might uncover simple arithmetic mistakes. You must have someone check every bill, and then follow-up any discrepancies. And this includes your telephone bill. This simple exercise, if done regularly as part of your business procedure, can certainly save you money and increase your profit.

Part 2

▮ Money

"It's now time to consider the group of profit-boosting strategies that are of a more financial nature, Charlie. You know, the things that accountants would typically be more familiar with."

"You mean things like pricing, costs, and budgets?"

I knew this was going to be more challenging, because Charlie, like most small business owners, was a hands-on type of person. And by that I mean he, like the vast majority, spends far too much time working *in* his business instead of *on* it. And he, like most, wouldn't have a clue about this area of his business—after all, isn't that why he has an accountant?

"You're on the right track, Charlie. But they're still areas of the business that the owner must have under control. They are nothing more than aspects of the business that are of a more financial nature and that again have a direct bearing on the profitability of the business."

"You mean just like what we've been discussing, except with a financial flavor?"

"That's exactly right. And there's nothing mystical or complicated about them either. It's just that I refer to them as being financial-type strategies, that's all. But let me explain by means of another real-life example."

He leaned back in his chair and closed his eyes. I knew he wasn't nodding off to sleep—he was getting comfortable and beginning to concentrate, just as a child does prior to listening to a favorite bedtime story.

"Tim and Natasha Roberts bought a men's clothing shop in Sydney back in 1999. Now neither of them knew the first thing about selling men's clothing at the time. They were full of enthusiasm and were keen to learn the tricks of the trade from the guy who had run the shop for the past 35 years. Tim soon discovered that, in doing so, he had become reliant on the 'old ways' of doing business."

Charlie was listening intently now, and nodded.

"For the first 15 months Tim relied on a bookkeeper to look after everything from paying the bills to doing the banking," I continued. I could tell Charlie could relate to the scenario. "She was also, you might say, his own secretary. This, of course, turned out to be a huge mistake. You see, although this bookkeeper did her work well, Tim never had a handle on the company's finances. He never knew the impact his cashflow problems were having on the business. In fact, he didn't even know he had a cashflow problem. And he certainly didn't know how much he owed suppliers or how much he had in the bank at any one time. He began to realize that he was spending all his time in the shop, concentrating on the physical aspects of selling only."

Charlie was beginning to shift around uncomfortably in his chair now. This story was definitely getting a little too close to home for comfort, I suspected.

"After the first 12 months, the excitement of owning a new business had well and truly worn off. The GST had been implemented and the Sydney Olympic Games were looming. Business was down, cashflow was pathetic, and Tim began to feel trapped. What's more, his wife Natasha had just delivered their first child and her maternity leave was about to run out. They had two choices: either she would go back to work or he'd have to build a place for her in the business. They chose the latter."

Charlie could sense I was getting to the exciting part.

"Natasha took charge of computerizing all the accounts in the business. This turned out to be the first of many steps they took to turn the business around. And it was the first time they could see every dollar being spent—and earned. You want to know what happened next?"

"Yeah, what?"

"They started to gain control of the business, and for the first time started to feel that it was theirs. You see, the bookkeeper decided to leave, and this gave Tim and Natasha real scope as far as the accounts were concerned. They could actually see that they were ordering too much in the way of stock. They also realized they were dealing with far too many suppliers. Things began to improve, and by the end of that financial year, they actually made a nice little profit. Tim put this down solely to the fact that the business was being managed better from a financial point of view."

Charlie sat up straight in his chair, turned to me, and said, "Was that all they needed to do to feel they were really in control of their business, Brad? I mean, it sounds sort of obvious, doesn't it?"

"Yes, it is, Charlie. But how many people continue blundering along without really coming to grips with the financial side of their business? It's almost as if they are scared of confronting the issue. But in reality, it's no big deal. Financial strategies are just like any other—it's just that they have more to do with 'money' and less to do with promotion, sales, advertising, or merchandising."

"But I'm not really good with figures, Brad."

"You don't need to be a mathematical wizard to make good financial decisions, Charlie. Rather, you need to be a good manager, and that comes with practice. But you're doing great so far. You'll soon see that dealing with strategies of a financial nature are no different than dealing with those designed to generate more leads for your business or to encourage repeat business. But let's not worry too much about this now. Rather let's jump in at the deep end and take a look at some of the financial strategies, shall we?"

What Are Money-Related Strategies?

How you manage the financial side of your business obviously affects the profits it will make. That goes without saying. But what do I mean when I talk about money-related strategies? Am I referring to investment strategies or different accounting systems or ways of keeping your books?

No, what I'm referring to here are strategies you'd use to *generate* more profit, not deal with it after it has been made.

Now, I know you can "make" more profit simply by changing the way you account for your money, but that's not really the object of what I'm suggesting. I'm talking about really making more profit—and hence more money—not smarter ways to make it appear as though your company is making more money.

I'm looking at this from a management point of view, not an accountant's. And this is what makes it doable, because you don't need to be a numbers person to make it happen—and you certainly don't need a financial degree. In fact, it's all the better if you don't!

So, to begin with, let's once again take a look at the word "money." What does it mean? And how does it relate to profit? According to the dictionary, it is a medium that can be exchanged for goods and services and is used as a measure of their values on the market. So far so good. But how does it relate to profit? Well, it also means profit or loss relating to money: *He made money on the sale of his properties.* Isn't that interesting?

The Strategies

Audit Costs and Set Budgets

It's really amazing how many businesses have no idea what their actual costs are. And some who believe that they know their costs usually only know the obvious ones like salaries, rent, materials, or stock on hand.

But that's only the tip of the iceberg. If you were to sit down and think about it, you'd soon realize that many of your costs are never actually measured or evaluated. How can you reduce them if you don't know what they are at present? How would you know if they were blowing out?

So take the time to find out what your actual costs are. Spend a whole week checking absolutely everything—and if you don't have the time or patience, hire someone to do it for you. It'll be well worth your while. You see, once you know what all your costs are, you can call around and get quotes from different suppliers for the things you spend money on regularly. You might be surprised at how much you're wasting. And remember, any savings here directly affects your profits.

Once you have done this, you need to think about setting monthly expenditure budgets. This is vitally important if you want your business to remain viable. See, by setting monthly budgets and sticking to them, you can ensure you're never in the position where you have more money going out than you have coming in.

But don't forget to let everyone know what the budgets are. How can they stick to them if they don't know what the limits are? Also stress that these budgets are *never* to be broken.

Remember DK Design Kitchens of Sydney? Well, it is a great example of what I'm talking about here.

When Coach Greg Albert asked the owners what their weekly or monthly sales were, they really couldn't tell him. Any Key Performance Indicators that he asked for, they also couldn't supply. This little exercise was a real awakening for them.

And as they didn't have a mission, vision, or culture statement in place, or even an organizational chart, they clearly had a lot of work to do. Needless to say, it took them quite a while to get through some of the ideas and suggestions that Greg gave them. Slowly it all came together. Greg was very patient, but kept pushing them forward. It got to the point where they really looked forward to the coaching calls. Then when they were able to supply the figures he asked for, it was very easy for the business to move forward. You see, they began to uncover a lot of things that needed tightening. And when they did, it added directly to their bottom line.

Increase Your Margins/Prices

Now I know this might sound simplistic, strange, or both, but if you want your profit to increase, the easiest way to achieve this is to increase your margins or your prices. It's that simple.

And the funny thing is that most business owners are too terrified to do this. They seem to believe it will drive them out of business! The exact opposite is true. You'll find that most of your customers won't even notice. And if they do, chances are they won't care. Those that do and object are probably your "C"- and "D"-Grade customers anyway. My experience is that it's business owners who have more of a problem with this strategy than their customers. So just do it.

You need to understand that this is the fastest and best way to bump up your profitability. But if you're too scared to increase your prices across the board, try doing it to just 80 percent of your range. Choose the slow movers first, increase their prices, and leave your fast sellers until last.

But let me give you a real-life example now. Live It Up Hairdressing in Sydney was your typical battling hairdressing salon—until they decided to take action. Owners Vance Fitzgerald and Renee Stuart wanted the business to improve. You see, while sales were running at $2300 a week, they had very little in the way of consistent marketing strategies, their team communication was very low, and there were no Key Performance Indicators. But they did have goals, which included increasing sales from approximately $2300 to $3000 a week within six months, and to obtain a better understanding of business.

All the ingredients were in place for them to begin working *on* the business in earnest. They had come to the realization that things just had to improve. Fortunately for them, they were also able to recognize their shortcomings, and decided to do something about it.

With the help of Coach Bernie Rorke, they began by concentrating first on drumming up more business. It's funny how many business owners instinctively want to *cut* prices to *increase* profit. This is something I never advocate. Pricing was increased by 10 percent and a new focus on the average dollar sale was introduced. They then began concentrating on ensuring that they exceeded their customer's expectations every time they visited. This was designed to not only make sure they returned, but that they referred their friends as well.

So what do you think the outcome of this strategy was? Turnover just about doubled, from $2300 a week to over $4000 a week within two months. That's nearly a 100 percent increase.

Profit also increased dramatically, enabling the owners to implement some improvements to their business, such as installing a computerized counter system and a new counter.

So don't write off this strategy without a further thought. Thousands of businesses I've coached have increased their prices without any negative effects. They all benefited immediately and marveled at the effect it had on their bottom line. So resist the temptation to give money away before you've even begun negotiating with clients or selling to customers. Don't do it.

Stop Discounting

Another brilliant strategy that will have an immediate effect on your bottom line is to stop discounting. Why give money away?

If you constantly discount, why bother having a regular retail price? Discounting not only costs you money, but it gives the impression that your normal prices are a ripoff. Think about those rug retailers who are always advertising massive discount sales. You know, up to 80 percent discount on all floor stock—final clearance sale—new stocks have just arrived, so old stock has to go. Trouble is, people become oblivious to all these sales after a while. They cease having an impact. They become no longer believable.

But perhaps what's worse, customers may hold off buying, thinking an item that's $100 today may only be $80 tomorrow. It's better not to discount at all but to simply offer more add-on value instead. You could consider something like the first service for free with each used car sold, or a free CD with every CD player bought. The idea is to add perceived value.

However, if your business routinely discounts, you might want to introduce this strategy as part of a repositioning of your business. That way your existing clientele won't view it with suspicion. You'll be able to introduce sweeping changes all at once.

Make It Easy to Buy

Before you can count the profit you're making, you need to have customers or clients in the first place. You need people to do business with you. Now, I know ensuring you do is a whole specialized field all its own (to find out more, read my books *Instant Leads, Instant Promotions, Instant Sales,* and *Instant Repeat Business*), but the point I'm making is that you need to make sure you're giving them every chance to do business with you. And because we are discussing financial strategies here, I'm suggesting you make it easy for people to deal with you from a financial point of view.

Why make this difficult by putting up financial barriers? If customers want to spend, help them, for goodness sake.

So how can you smooth the path to the proverbial cash register?

Simple. Here's how:

- Allow payment terms or financing options. You could make arrangements with a bank or credit company, or you could run your own credit facility, allowing customers to pay you off over a period of time. This allows your customers to spend more by giving them the chance to pay it off over time. You'll find this is particularly beneficial if you're up-selling them to a product that's beyond their original budget. And if you were smart, you'd want to reap maximum benefit from your new finance facility. How, you ask? Simple. Approach a number of lending institutions and offer to sell their products to your customers for a commission. This is a great way to further boost your profits. You can also charge interest on 30, 60, or 90-day accounts, but offer a discount if they are paid within seven days. That will ensure you can deposit their money in your bank sooner.

- Allow Eftpos (electronic funds transfer at point of sale), checks, and credit cards. This is one of the most important facilities you can offer. It can increase your average dollar sale by allowing customers to spend more than they have in their wallet at the time. Credit cards in particular are helpful if you're trying to up-sell or on-sell. If they can have the better model and not have to pay for it right away, they'll take it more often than not. And remember, there are many customers out there who simply would not be able to buy things if it weren't for credit. This is particularly true for higher-priced or nonessential items. Having credit card facilities is important for another reason: Many more affluent customers charge everything to their credit card because it gives them 55 interest-free days as well as loyalty reward points that can be redeemed for goods and services at a later date. They make use of this facility because that way they are able to get the best leverage from their money. It really does make good financial sense.

- Allow trade-ins or trade-ups. By allowing trade-ins you solve your customers' problem of what to do with the old product. It will also give them the chance to fit that new purchase into their budget. Offering trade-ins means you have the chance to up-sell them a better model. It's also a way of making a more expensive item seem affordable. And while you're at it, why not offer home delivery? Charging a fee for this service is a great way to increase your average dollar sale. This can prove very popular with larger items such as home furnishings.

- Allow layaway. This is a great way to get people to buy products that they can't really afford right then and to increase your average dollar sale at the same time. It has the added advantage of bringing them into your store on a regular basis to make payments. Obviously this gives you the chance to show them any new products that you can attempt to sell to them. In any event, they probably would need other products in the meantime, so show them what else you have. Let them know what you stock. Show them your entire range. So often I've had business owners tell me that customers buy one item from them, then they go on to buy accessories for that item from a competitor, simply because they didn't realize the accessories were stocked by the original sellers.

Reorganize Your Financial Affairs

Now that we've looked at what you can do financially to assist people to deal with you, the next logical thing to do is to look at steps you can take within your own business to help keep as much money in the business as possible.

Now, I know this may sound like a stupid or obvious statement, but you'd be surprised at how many people don't realize that for a business to make a profit, its outgoings must be less than its incomings.

Of course, there are lots of things you can do to achieve this, like putting more effort into the sales process, but I'm focusing here on those steps that are more financial in nature.

The first thing you should do is to reduce all your costs by 10 percent. This may not be easy, but with a little effort and planning it should be possible. But before you can do this, you must know what your costs are right now. How else will you know whether you've managed to reach this target or not?

Of course, it will be easier to reduce some costs than others. That's fine. And don't stress out too much if you just can't seem to cut them all. You see, the important thing to remember is that lower overhead means greater profits, so you really do need to devote some time to this area.

You'd be surprised what you can achieve just by going through the exercise of phoning around for a few quotes on some of the more routine things you do, or basic supplies your business consumes. In today's competitive environment, you should easily be able to achieve a savings on most items or services. So phone your suppliers, subcontractors, or freight service providers, and see if you can do better.

Don't be too impatient here. Take it one step at a time. If you can reduce your total costs by just 1 percent each week, that's fine. After 10 weeks, you'll be in good shape. Break down each area of your business into manageable parts (it could be along departmental lines or according to each work area) and attack them individually. And when you've reached your target, don't sit back and relax. Constantly audit all facets of your operation to ensure your savings are maintained. It's no use allowing things to slip back to what they were previously; that will just sap your newfound profit.

If you find this too difficult to attempt personally, consider bringing in an outsider to do it for you. This could have benefits, especially as far as unemotional objectivity is concerned.

Now, have a good hard look at the number of business loans you have. See if you can consolidate them into one new loan. The advantage of doing this is you only have to pay one amount of interest and one repayment. Of course, you'll be looking for a loan with a better rate of interest than you currently have. But don't confine your attention to the interest rate alone. Look too at whatever other features and benefits the facility has to offer. You see, the cheapest need not necessarily mean the best. You could come up with four or five deals that all have a lower interest rate than you're currently saddled with, but one of them might offer other benefits, like an additional line of credit or lower fees.

And when you've found one, don't sit back and relax. Keep your finger on the pulse by regularly shopping around for a better deal. The least that will happen is you'll find you still have the best deal available. And don't restrict yourself to traditional banks. Sometimes nonbank lenders and credit unions offer better deals. Also offer your chosen institution all your banking needs. That might just sweeten them enough to provide you with an exceptional deal.

Once you've sorted out your loan accounts, turn your attention to reducing your accounts from 30-day terms to 7 days. This will immediately allow you to earn additional interest on incoming cash to purchase more stock, pay for updated pieces of equipment or other income-generating items. It will allow you to make your money work harder for you. Improving your cashflow is the name of the game. In any event, it's always better to have this money sitting in your bank account rather than in someone else's. Reward customers who pay early, but by the same token, charge interest to those who pay late. Your accounting system should be able to alert you immediately to payments that are in arrears. If it doesn't, then get one that does.

Have a good, hard look to see whether you can pay cash for things you need instead of using credit. When you think about it, any interest you are currently paying on loans is wasted money. I realize sometimes you need credit. Often it's something you can't do without, but if you can, it will certainly benefit your bottom line.

Paying cash for as much as you can has another important benefit. It allows you to keep your overhead to a minimum. Trust me, in a slow month the one thing you really don't want is fixed monthly costs. The biggest killer of small business has got to be the signing of long-term contracts that add to monthly fixed overhead. Many business owners justify this by thinking it at least allows them to purchase items they otherwise wouldn't be able to afford. They reason that as the cost is spread out over a long period of time, they'll easily be able to pay it off faster than required because it will bring success sooner than was otherwise possible. This seldom happens. Pay cash for as many larger purchases as you can, even if it means buying secondhand.

If you have business loans, aim to pay them off as soon as you can. This might take time, but you'll benefit in the long run. Consider consolidating your loans so you can pay off only one, and at a new, negotiated (lower) interest rate. And if you use a company credit card, look at it as a convenience, not a source of long-term capital.

Talking about credit cards, you can save a bundle by using a 55-day interest-free company credit card instead of paying for everything by check. You see, this way you not only save on bank fees and charges, you also get to leave your money in your bank for an additional 55 days, earning interest during that time. Or you can use it in the meantime on other investments. After a while you'll also have accumulated enough bonus points to save yourself having to pay for airfares or other items, which at the end of the day equates to more profit for you. Another advantage, and potential profit-booster, is that you'll have a regular record of all your expenditure—all compiled by your bank! Yes, statements can be wonderful things.

What Else?

Of course, there are all sorts of other things you can do of a financial nature to improve your bottom line. Here's a list of some for you to consider:

- You could reduce the cost of your team by putting your salespeople on a commission-only system. That way you won't lose money through team members taking time off when they're sick, tired, or just plain lazy. You'd also save money over holiday periods and by not having to fund unproductive times like lunch hours or Friday afternoon slow periods. The upside (for the salespeople) is that they will earn more if they perform better. Offer outstanding rates of commission. You see, nothing motivates like money.

- You could also consider renegotiating employment agreements. This allows you to dispense with overtime pay and coordinating vacations—something that will quickly add money to your bottom line. But remember to make sure your new deal is seen as worthwhile; otherwise, you won't attract the right sort of person to work for you.

- If your business is small, consider joining forces with other small businesses to form a buying group. The idea is quite simple. Large suppliers offer bulk discounts to businesses that buy a lot. Take advantage of this by joining forces with other businesses and in so doing, combining your purchasing power. This will allow substantial savings in a short period of time. And those savings, of course, go directly to your bottom line.

- Invest as much as you can in automated equipment and sell off obsolete equipment or machinery. You'll be surprised at how much extra revenue this will generate.

- Remember to reduce or eliminate taxation expenses. What do I mean by this? No, I'm not going to go into this here, because this is where we become bogged down in financial and taxation concepts. What I would suggest, however, is that you get yourself a *good* accountant—one who's financially literate (and just because he's qualified as an accountant doesn't automatically mean that he is.) There are many things an accountant can do to minimise your tax burden, so it's really worth your while finding a good one. And it's usually worth paying the extra he might charge.

- And while we're talking tax, rent for maximum tax write-offs. Let me explain it this way: If you own the building you work in, it's classed as an asset and can't be claimed. However, if you were to rent it instead, it would become an expense, which you could claim. Understand that anything you can save on your tax bill will help make your business more profitable. Computer equipment, cars, and other rapidly depreciating items are excellent rental candidates. So, forget the notion that rent is "dead money," as it can provide you with significant tax savings.

- Another thing you should be doing is checking to see that your accounts are sent out regularly and on time. Send out 7-day accounts as soon as the job is complete or the product has been delivered. The same applies to 30-day accounts.

- Complete your weekly or monthly profit and loss reports as soon as you can, as this is a great barometer for telling you whether you are making money or not. Remember this: You cannot manage what you cannot measure.

- Work out your costs as a percentage of sales, as this will give you an idea of how many sales you need to make before you start showing a profit. To do this, work out how much it costs you to run your business each week. You need to include all expenses, from wages to stationery, electricity bills to rent—anything that you have to pay to keep your doors open. Then work out how many sales are needed to cover that cost before you start to see a profit. Once you've identified this figure, explain to your team what is required to keep the business profitable. This will motivate team members to increase sales and achieve their goals.

- Charge for offering a finance facility. This is a great way to increase your profits from each sale. So if you offer financing to your customers, you should arrange it on a commission basis. Approach a number of loan companies and offer to sell their loan product for a commission. Another way of earning money for credit is to simply charge interest on 30, 60, or 90-day accounts. Offer a discount for accounts paid within 7 days. This means that any account that isn't paid in that time is loaded with interest.

- Negotiate fixed rates for services you regularly use. For example, if you need to have computers serviced four times a month, at $120 per service, it would be worthwhile arranging to pay a retainer of $160 per month and $60 per service. This can be applied to any regular service you use.

- Charge for postage or delivery. Recovering your costs in this area will add handsomely to your bottom line, and best of all, most people now accept this as a legitimate cost in this "user-pays" society. Doing business over the Internet or through mail order is now commonplace, so why should you be out of pocket if you don't already recover this expense from your customers?

- Charge consulting fees. Many businesses offer free advice on a wide range of topics, yet there is a whole new area waiting to be tapped into, and that's consulting. You see, by charging for your advice, you place yourself into a whole new business category. And there are distinct benefits for you here too. You see, if customers pay for advice, they're likely to value it all the more. They're also likely to act on it. This strategy may not be applicable to every situation, but if it is to yours, it can become a whole new profit center.

$$\boxed{\textbf{Part 3}}$$

∎ Marketing

"This brings us to the group of strategies that most people would immediately recognize, Charlie. It's time to take a closer look at marketing-related things we can do to add to the profitability of a business."

"Now you're talking, Brad. This, I think, is an area I'm more comfortable with."

I knew this would get his attention.

"Marketing is usually the first thing people think of when I begin talking about ways of boosting profit. I suppose it's because they relate sales to marketing, and probably because it's the activity directly related to that exchange that happens when product changes hands for money. But the strange thing is that, in actual fact, most businesses don't concentrate enough of their attention on marketing. They focus more of their attention on the distribution side of the business. Way more, in fact."

Charlie was interested and listened intently.

"The fact of the matter is that distribution and marketing are both equally important. You've got to put 50 percent of your time, effort, and investment into getting your products or services to the market and the other half getting the market to come to your products or services. The challenge is that most business owners put about 90 percent of their time and resources into distribution and only about 10 percent into marketing. The fact of the matter is that you've got to market if you're ever going to make real money."

It was now time to get down to business. I could tell Charlie was itching to get into the specifics. So it was time for another example.

"Remember that Men's Clothing Store I was telling you about earlier? Well, let's go back there for a moment to find out how marketing strategies turned that business around."

"Yes, I'd be interested to hear what worked for them and the effect it had on their business," Charlie responded.

"Remember when I outlined how Tim and Natasha had taken control of their business, The Club Shoppe, by becoming intimately involved with its finances? Well, their Coach then got them to become more proactive from a marketing point of view as well. All of a sudden, instead of just plodding along and wishing for customers to come in through the door, they started deliberately going after them. They started a frequent buyer's program that rewarded customers every time they bought, with points that could be redeemed at a later stage for goods from the shop."

"I know what you mean, Brad. It's a clever way of building up your repeat business and encouraging customer loyalty at the same time, isn't it?"

Charlie and I had previously discussed how to stimulate repeat business at length and in some detail. To find out more, read my book *Instant Repeat Business*.

"Tim began to compile specific customer lists that grouped people together according to their likes and dislikes. This enabled him to plan promotions for each individual group and to make contact with each group specifically. For example, he organized a 'Made-to-Measure' suit and jacket promotion and was able to reach his target market because he had a list of people who had an interest in Made-to-Measure articles."

Marketing is such a wide and varied field, and as we were discussing marketing strategies designed specifically to improve profitability—not all are—I knew it would be more effective to explain what I meant by way of a general, and real, example.

"Tim then reached an agreement with Lavazza Coffee whereby he would serve their coffee to his customers, if that company supplied him the coffee and an espresso machine free of charge. Wasn't that clever? Anyway, he also had wine and whiskey for those customers who had had a particularly difficult day at work. And do you know what? Some customers began coming in just to say hello and to have a cup of tea. Wasn't that great?"

I could tell that Charlie's mind was racing. These are exactly the types of things that would appeal to him.

"Now for the really exciting part. Tim invited even the local Harley Davidson dealer to put a bike on display in the shop. He told me it was great to see these 'shopped-out' husbands dragging their wives into the store just to see the Harley, and to hear their wives say, 'Yeah sure, but you need some new clothes!' Work had truly become fun."

The mere mention of the words "Harley Davidson" made Charlie sit up straight. He swung around and faced me square on.

"The Coach warned Tim that other shop owners would think him a bit weird, and he was dead right. In fact, there was a time when center traffic was slow and the other shop owners began complaining about this. The Club Shoppe was booming. They kept asking Tim how he did it, and he always told them to get a coach. You see, Tim had found that during his first six months of coaching, his turnover increased by 18 percent, but more importantly, his profit had increased by nearly 40 percent."

I just love watching people's reactions when I quote startling profit increases. You see, when discussing business, there's nothing quite as dramatic as real-life examples because they are things people can relate to.

"When it came time for them to launch the new season's clothing line, Tim wanted to try something a little different. A new James Bond movie was showing in town and he thought it would be great if he could get James Bond into the store for the promotion. Well, unfortunately Pierce Brosnan was busy that weekend, so he organized an Aston Martin DB7 to be on display in the shop instead. Not only that, he went further and organized complimentary dinners at the MG Garage Restaurant for his customers."

I was now talking Charlie's language. He was loving it, and it showed. So I pressed on.

"Needless to say, the promotion was a huge success. What Tim had succeeded in doing was taking positive and imaginative steps to ensure his profits increased dramatically. Not acceptably, *dramatically*."

Charlie was impressed and wanted to hear more.

"What else did Tim do, Brad? I just know there has to be more."

"You're not wrong, Charlie. Tim had realized that looking after his profit was all about going the extra mile. He started doing things he knew nobody else would be doing, like sending new customers thank-you gifts for coming into the shop, or sending his good customers gifts such as pen sets or calculators."

That raised Charlie's eyebrows. I pretended not to notice, and continued.

"I remember his telling me about a lady who came into the store and began looking around. He introduced himself and struck up a conversation. She had never been into the store before, even though she was a local. She told him that her husband shopped at one of their competitors about 12 miles away. So Tim took her address and her husband's name. When she left, he boxed up a pen and pencil set and promptly sent it to her. That weekend she and her husband came into the shop and spent over $6000. They went on to become dedicated customers."

I fell silent for a few moments, eager for the impact of the story to sink in.

"Brad, that's a very powerful lesson," he said at length. "I can see how I can adapt some of those strategies for my own business."

"Yes, Charlie, and the beauty of all this is that it's really so simple. There's no rocket science here at all. Now let's have a closer look at these profit-building strategies that are more of a marketing nature, shall we?"

What Are Marketing-Related Strategies?

When it comes to sales and marketing, there are a number of excellent strategies you can use to increase your profit. No, I'm not talking about salesmanship here—you know, the tricks and techniques salespeople use to help steer a prospect toward a buying decision. What I'm talking about are tactical decisions taken by the business owner (or management) that relate directly to the sales function. These are decisions relating to what salespeople should do in order to ensure maximum profit for the business.

Still confused? Don't worry. From what I've seen, so are the majority of business owners out there. But rest assured, by the time you finish reading this chapter, you'll have all the knowledge required to ensure your business maximizes its potential as far as profit is concerned. You see, these strategies are so simple, yet very powerful, and that's the beauty of it. They're easy to implement and guaranteed to transform your bottom line.

Once again, let's take a quick look at what the word "marketing" actually means. According to the dictionary, it is defined as "the commercial functions involved in transferring goods from producer to consumer." I think that's pretty well understood, don't you? So where does the word come from and what are its roots? It actually comes from the Vulgar Latin word *marcatus,* which itself was derived from the Latin word *mercatus.* The past participle of *mercari* means "to buy," and the word *merx* means "merchandise." To buy merchandise. Isn't that interesting? You see, the word had to do with the intentions of the *buyer,* not the *seller.* And that's largely the perspective modern-day marketers *should* take.

The Strategies

Up-Sell

This can be done in situations where you have a basic and deluxe version of a particular product. It works by selling your customers a more expensive version of the product they're looking at, based on its benefits. When up-selling, it's important to explain how the more expensive model will better suit their long-term needs.

So how do you go about achieving this? Make sure you spell out clearly the long-term benefits of the more expensive item. And don't forget to put the higher price into perspective. This is very important. You could explain that it might be a little costlier now, but in the long run it'll be much cheaper. Reliability, longevity, and performance are usually important benefits any deluxe model has over the more basic one. But don't overdo the up-selling job, as your customers might have good reason for wanting the basic model. They might be on a very tight budget, for instance, in which case the last thing you want is to put them off buying altogether. Beware of painting such a rosy picture for the deluxe model that you, in fact, write off the basic model. Don't play the one off against the other because you then run the risk of losing the sale altogether if the customer absolutely doesn't want the more expensive option. Gain a smaller margin (and profit) than none at all. Keep a fine balance when up-selling, and be alert to any signals your customer is giving during the up-selling process.

Cross or Add-on Sell

This is a strategy that is successfully used by many large companies all over the world. Take McDonald's, for instance. Whenever a customer walks up to the counter and says, "Can I have a Big Mac, please," the attendant always responds, "And would you like a medium or a small serving of fries with that?" They never miss an opportunity to sell you more. And guess what? Many times the answer will be, "Yes, give me a medium, please." But if the answer is "no," they haven't lost anything anyway.

Cross- or add-on selling can be very effective when selling products or services that are used in conjunction with others. A good example of this would be selling your customers a watering system when they buy a quantity of lawn seed. Or try buying a suit without the sales assistant asking you to try some ties. You can also cross-sell associated products or services on a commission basis with another company.

When applying this strategy, always offer more than the customers are looking for. And offer them a package deal if they buy something else as well. Take every opportunity to clinch the deal, as every sale you make adds towards your profitability. But avoid overpressurizing people. After all, you do want them to come back and do business with you again. Remember, it generally takes two-and-a-half sales to customers before they become profitable—and that's our aim, isn't it?

Down-Sell

If you can't up-sell, cross-sell or add-on sell to a customer, then you still have one option left, and that's to down-sell. You see, your aim here is to sell them something. Look at it this way: Whenever a customer leaves your premises after spending money, it's money in your bank. But whenever they leave without spending, it's a lost opportunity.

If you show them the higher-priced item first, then the one priced below the one they originally had in mind will seem extremely cheap. This can be a really effective strategy when your customer definitely can't afford a more expensive item and probably can't quite afford the one they originally had in mind either.

A good example here is real estate. It's a common tactic in the industry to begin showing prospective buyers properties priced about 20 percent above that which they say they can afford before down-selling, if that doesn't work. This strategy works well because quite often buyers start off being a little too optimistic, and when they realize just what the mortgage repayments will be on higher-priced properties, they quickly lower their price expectations. Real estate salespeople then show them properties that are priced lower than the range they asked for. This works particularly well by showing them properties in a neighboring (and lower priced) suburb. "See what you can get here for a little less money," they say. "You get far better quality, more rooms, larger grounds and more convenience—and all for $20,000 less than in the suburb you were originally inquiring about."

Rather than attempting to sell them only a higher-priced item, and as a result losing the sale altogether, you simply sell them a similar product that fits just below their original budget.

You need to remember a few important things if you decide to down-sell. Wait until you are absolutely sure your up-selling isn't working before launching headlong into down-sell mode—you might just up-sell each time! But if you have to down-sell, try and make it sound as though there is little difference between the two products anyway. And if you simply don't have another product that is cheaper—if down-selling isn't an option—then aim at selling them something else altogether.

Whatever you do, try to ensure that you put money in the cash register at every opportunity.

Make Use of Lists

Lists can be very effective sales tools if used correctly. So what are lists, you ask? And is there more than one type? You bet.

- The first is the *checklist*. It's used to achieve similar results to add-on selling; you simply run through a checklist with your clients whenever they purchase a particular type of product. This list should be prepared in advance and used with as many different products as possible. For example, if you run a hardware store and a customer comes in to buy a can of paint, you or one of your team should run through the checklist with the customers to see if they need brushes, thinners, drop sheets, stirrers, etc. You see, if they are planning on doing a bit of painting around the house over the weekend, chances are they'll need more than just the paint. And if they do and you don't see to it that they buy these items from you, chances are they'll buy them from another store. You simply can't paint without a brush, paint tray, or cleanup material to go with the paint.

Make sure every member of your team has the checklist and knows how to use it. Consistency is the name of the game. You see, if you're getting mediocre results while using checklists, how will you know whether it's your checklist that needs refining or another element of your marketing mix? Constantly test and measure your results, and if need be, alter, change, or fine-tune your checklist until it produces the results you want it to.

And, of course, the checklist needs to be used with *every* customer. A great way to ensure it is being used by everyone every time a customer shops is to have a reward system in place that acknowledges team members who make *additional* sales from the list. Bear in mind that it's all about making additional sales, as these are the ones that dramatically affect your bottom line. Remember, it takes two-and-a-half sales to any one customer before you begin to make a profit from him. So make this happen as soon as you can by making those two-and-a-half sales during the first visit if at all possible. That way you'll be operating extremely efficiently and profitably.

- To take the checklist idea a little further, why not turn your checklist into an actual *shopping list*? Then have your shopping list nicely laid out and printed and handed to your customers. You see, the idea is to provide them with a list of items they may need to complete a particular project. You'll find this strategy most effective with hardware stores, photography stores, golf stores, and the like. Stationery stores could produce a "back to school" shopping list. This would be extremely effective especially if they had consulted with schools in the area to find out everything scholars are required to buy.

Remember to keep the list brief. Only include items with mass appeal. Offer a package deal if they buy more than, say, three items on the list. And resist the temptation to simply use the list to itemize those things you currently have on sale. You need to explain the benefits each provides. Finally, include your contact details and a call to action. Many people will take the list home, so you need to ensure they remember where it came from.

- Very often it takes more than good salesmanship and a checklist or shopping list to make a sale. You may need to go further. You may need to dig as deep as you can. If so, then make sure you ask enough questions to leave no stone unturned. This is where having a great *questionnaire* comes in. The more questions you ask, the more chance you have of finding another need or want that you can fill.

Also, if you're unsure of what additional products or services that you could sell to a customer, resorting to the questionnaire can be an effective way of finding out. Use it to ask your customers what else they would like you to sell them. Don't limit yourself too much. Ask the customers to get a little creative—who knows, there could be a whole new opportunity just waiting to be uncovered.

Make your questionnaire simple but effective as a sales tool. Don't bog customers down with overly long and involved questions—after all it's not a survey you're conducting. You're probing for another sales opportunity. Offer customers an incentive to participate. And let them know why you're asking them these questions. Make sure they understand that it's ultimately to help them. Fill out the questionnaire on the spot. Act as a sounding board as you dig deeper. With practice you'll quickly get the hang of this. And don't be afraid to ask for their suggestions—you may be very surprised at what you'll hear. Then act quickly. Let me give you an example:

The most common complaint I get today from small to medium business owners is that they can't compete with the big guys on price. The perception in the marketplace is that people are shopping on price alone. The only reason your customers ask the price up-front is because that is what we, as business owners, have trained them to do.

How many times have you called or gone into a business not really knowing what model, style, color, or features you were looking for, and purely asked for the price? At this point, did the salesperson come back with, "That is $29.95," or did they ask you some questions about what you were looking to use the product or service for? In this instance, let's say you wanted to buy a kettle.

Now, in most people's eyes, a kettle is a kettle, even though they may have many different features and offer the user many different benefits.

So what if the salesperson simply said to you when you inquired about price, "Just so I can help you better, is it OK if I ask you a couple of questions about the kettle you are looking for?" Would you have answered "yes?" My bet is that the answer would have most definitely been "yes!"

The salesperson could then ask questions like:

- "Are you looking to replace an existing kettle or is it a gift for someone?"
- "Do you regularly use your kettle or is it rarely used?"
- "Would you like a kettle with a quick boiling time?"
- "Have you seen the cordless options that are available?"
- "Are you looking for something to match your kitchen?"
- "So what color are you looking for?"
- "Is it important that it has an automatic cutoff after the kettle has boiled?"
- "Are you after a stove-top option or an electric kettle?"
- "Kettles come in different cup capacities; do you require 10-cup capacity or is 5 a better size for you?"

From these questions the customers get the idea that the salesperson is genuinely interested in their needs and is able to offer options concerning the most suitable kettles to meet their needs. The question of price is therefore negated. It is just a matter of now asking the customers to buy.

A good salesperson would then ask, "Well, based on what we have just spoken about, there are two options to choose from: model X and model Y. Which one suits you best? Great, I can either put that away for now or I can process it on credit card. Which do you prefer?"

This example was based on a kettle—a relatively small dollar item—but how does this apply to your business? This process works equally well for cars, houses, furniture, service-based businesses, and any other product I can think of, including funeral homes. You just need to work out what your customers are actually looking for when they inquire about the price. Try and uncover what's more important to them in their buying decision!

Offer Great Value

Offering exceptional value has got to be one of the best ways to ensure that your cash registers keep ringing. Understand this: although *profit* is the name of the game, it's *cashflow* that is the lifeblood of business.

It's cashflow that ensures there's enough money flowing through the veins of the business to enable a profit to be made.

So think of it from a customer's point of view. If you wanted or needed to buy a particular item, which you knew to be widely available, what would make you buy from Business A instead of from Business B? Well, all sorts of things, really, but I'd bet price was right up there near the top of the list.

OK, let's assume this item was similarly priced at a dozen different businesses. What then would persuade you to buy from one and not the others? Probably convenience. Now this is something that's largely beyond your control as a business owner. You could shift to a more convenient location, but generally speaking, this isn't really an option because if you were conveniently situated for one customer, chances are you won't be for another. So let's leave this one alone. It's a red herring.

What would the next determining factor be for you, the itchy shopper with money burning a hole in his pocket, waiting to be spent? I bet it's probably great customer service, familiarity with the business and its people, loyalty, or other marketing-related factors.

Now here's how you can rearrange this priority list and get potential customers to do business with you instead:

- Create *package deals*. This is an excellent way to move more items, increase your average dollar sale, and boost your profits. What you are basically doing is offering product at a group rate to customers who buy as part of a package deal. How do you achieve this? Simply package up a number of associated products and sell them at a price that is lower than they cost individually, but higher than your average dollar sale. Always see if you can group complimentary products together, like car wash and a sponge, or hair shampoo and conditioner. The trick is to try and include products that don't sell as well on their own. Sponges and conditioner are good illustrations of this. Package deals are also a great strategy to use if you need to sell slow-moving items. But do make them time sensitive. You don't want potential customers to procrastinate forever before making up their minds. After all, while your aim is to get money in the bank, you really want it in your bank sooner rather than later.

- Another way of giving your customers great value is to create great *bulk buy* deals. It's an old strategy, but a good one. What you're effectively doing is enticing your customers to buy more than they really need at that time.

  It's great for customers too, especially if your offer involves product that they have to use anyway, as they'll be benefiting from buying at a discounted price. Consumables spring immediately to mind. Getting them to stock up now, rather than spreading their purchasing over the next few months, provides you with certain advantages. First, you tie them up as customers in the medium term. They no longer become prospects for your opposition, who might sway them over down the road through special offers, promotions, etc. Secondly, getting their money in your bank now means you can make use of it for other things like buying more stock in bulk (and saving), paying for an equipment upgrade, or financing some other form of investment. At the very least you'll be able to earn interest on the money by letting it sit in the bank. Oh, and one other thing: Do ensure that you actually offer a reduced price for the bulk deal. Customers are very smart. If they feel they have been hoodwinked, you'll lose them forever. But in offering a great price, make sure you don't compromise your margins. It is profit you're chasing, you know.

- A variation on the bulk buy theme is to offer customers a gift if they spend over a certain amount. For example, they could get a free lesson when they buy a set of golf clubs priced at over $400. Remember this: the gift shouldn't cost you much—you are aiming at maximizing your profit—but it should appear to the customer that it's a great deal. It's all about perceived value here. And don't forget to advertise the fact that you're giving away gifts. This in itself will act as a great lead-generation tool as well.

- Again, you can develop variations on the theme here, such as giving customers *incentives for bigger purchases*. Offer points or give out funny money for each dollar spent. When your clients reach a certain number of points they can receive a discount off their next purchase. Funny money can be honored as real money that is then used for future purchases, or as mentioned before, you can give a gift with a purchase greater than a certain set dollar value. The idea is to get your customers to spend more than they normally would just to earn extra points. And don't be afraid of always having incentives in place to entice people to buy up. It's far cheaper than advertising for new customers. This strategy also allows you to build an element of fun into your daily routine. Not only will your sales team appreciate it, your customers too will enjoy the experience and remember it long afterwards. A secondary advantage of this is top-of-mind awareness, which will do much to ensure that you enjoy repeat business. It will also benefit your bottom line. They might also tell their friends about their shopping experience. This is, of course, one of the best forms of lead generation you could wish for.

- And don't forget to give your team *incentives for making bigger sales*. You see, achieving sales of bigger value is something you should be pursuing from both ends of the business spectrum—your customers and your sales team. Why just concentrate on one-half of the equation? Set targets for your team and offer a bonus of some kind for each one that is achieved. List the different prizes up for grabs beside each goal. Running this strategy over the course of a month will keep their enthusiasm running high. A free Christmas party or social club function could be great incentives as team goals. Make it fun. Monitor on a chart how team members are progressing each week. This will help to get everyone involved.

We all know that everyone likes a bargain. The flip side to that is this: If customers can't get a bargain, they at least want great value. Looking at this from your point of view, giving customers a bargain usually means sacrificing margin. And this, as we all know, means less profit. Now sometimes settling for less profit is preferable to no profit at all, but the general aim of this book is to ensure you achieve *increased* profits in your business.

So if we don't want to give away margin, what can we do?

- Give them *added value*. Make no mistake, offering added value encourages people to buy from you. What I'm talking about here are things like a free first service with each used car sold, or half-priced scotch guarding on lounge suites. Try offering these on the deluxe models only as a way to entice your customers to buy up and spend more.

- As a business owner or manager, your job is to find cheap ways to add value to your current product lineup. And when I say "cheap," I mean cheap in financial terms, not in quality. You see, you want people to buy from you without your first having to offer up some of the profit you stand to make through each transaction. Don't give away what you don't have to. It's all about *perceived value* here. For instance, something that to you may have no monetary value at all. It could be two tickets to attend a top sporting event. If you had a sponsorship arrangement in place with the sports team, you could receive a set of free tickets. These tickets might ordinarily be very expensive or not generally available, yet highly sought after. They would then be offered to anyone who bought a new car or overseas holiday package, for instance. The general rule here is, the more expensive the product, the more you offer.

Understand that giving away something of perceived value is all about giving away the *value* of an item, not its hard cost to you.

- Of course there are many other ways to get people to buy more than they really need. There are the *three-for-the-price-of-two* offers, *four-for-the-price-of-three* offers, and *buy-one-get-one-free* offers. When contemplating these, make sure the margins are there to make them profitable. Alternatively, see if you can pass the costs on to your suppliers. They may have promotional budgets to back up strategies like these. Also, use these promotions as pullers. Once people are interested, see if you can sell them something else at the same time. You could also use them to clear slow-moving stock or discontinued lines.

- While we're concentrating on value, there's another thing you really have to do, and that's to *educate your customers on value, not price*. This is vital for any business to do because it's a strategic activity that addresses one of the core issues of profitability. You see, most customers instinctively look for the best price they can get. If you allow them to continue in this mode, you will eventually go broke. The main goal of businesspeople *must* be profit—not turnover, number of clients, or even increasing the size of their business. It's *profit*. And price-cutting, discounting, or whatever else you want to call it is the antithesis of profit. Therefore, businesspeople should be fundamentally opposed to the notion of discounting—they should regard it with nothing less than revulsion.

Hard words, I know, but you have to look after your profits first. Now there may be occasions when you will want to discount, and those we've already discussed. If discounting forms part of your marketing plans, then that's something else entirely. But discounting just because a customer wants it or asks for it is just not right. Don't let your customers believe it's OK to demand a discount. Get them out of the habit right away. You need to get your customers focused on the benefits of the product and not the price. This is very important when dealing with bargain hunters or when selling higher priced or luxury items. To use this strategy effectively, skip over your customers' price queries by immediately coming back at them with a benefit.

Ask People to Buy Some More

This technique is probably the most simple to use. When your customers make a purchase, ask them if they would like to buy a couple of spares to have on hand. This works well with disposable items like shoelaces or light bulbs. You'll get the best results with this technique if the items you're selling are about to increase in price.

This technique also really works. Just ask any successful salesperson. When customers have finally made up their minds to buy a particular item, and after they've been through the rigmarole of comparing it with alternatives, haggling over price, and generally emerging from the sales process unscathed, chances are they've built up a good rapport with the salesperson. This is, of course, particularly true with higher-priced items like houses and cars. Anyway, once they've signed on the dotted line or parted with their cash, they usually experience a certain level of euphoria and satisfaction. And then, during those precious moments after the deal has been done and when they are feeling particularly proud of the way they secured the best possible deal for themselves, when the salesperson asks, in a friendly tone, whether they should consider buying a few accessories to enhance the functionality or usefulness of their purchase, what do they usually say? "Of course, why not?" Or, "If you really think so, sure." Or, "And how much extra will that cost? Oh, that's not bad—yes, add that in."

It's all about making those extra few sales that you wouldn't otherwise have made. And when you really think about it, getting someone who has just bought to buy something extra makes good sense from a marketing point of view because all the hard work has already been done. You won't have to start out afresh looking for new leads, then spending time, money, and effort building rapport and converting them into customers. It's already been done. All you need to do is pop the question. If they say no, you've lost nothing. You won't even lose face as you could easily brush it off in a jocular fashion by saying, "That's OK. Just thought you might be interested."

What Else?

There are a number of other strategies you could consider. Remember, every little bit helps, as the effects of profit-building strategies are cumulative. Lots of little savings add up to something quite respectable. Here are some ideas to consider:

- Sell through direct mail and the Internet. This is a great way to lower overheads and other expenses such as wages and advertising costs. By using these mediums you're able to operate from home, simply taking orders and mailing out the goods. Selling by mail order reduces your overhead, giving you a much bigger slice of the profits.

- Sell through multilevel marketing or party plans. This also allows you to operate from home with minimal overhead. You're effectively recruiting people to sell your product for you, without having to pay them a wage. You also travel to their homes so you don't need to spend money turning your home into an office.

- If you run a store or shop, place impulse items like chocolates or magazines at cash registers to tempt people as they wait. The longer they wait the greater chance of their weakening. Impulse buys can also be placed throughout the store. For example, place flashlights next to batteries, mops with buckets, and paintbrushes with paint. Impulse buys increase your average dollar sale, which in turn increases your ultimate profit level.

- Increase your chances of finalizing the deal or sale by asking your clients if they would like either the red one or the blue one—delivery on Wednesday or Thursday—if they'll pay by check or credit card. Always give people a choice between one way and another, and never ask a question that can be answered by a yes or no, because chances are they'll say "no." Assume they're going to buy; just ask a detail-oriented question to confirm their purchase.

- The more your customers know about your full product and service list, the more they will buy. Place signs around your business to inform your customers of the things you do. Include this information in your mail outs, newsletters, and telephone-on-hold messages. It is also important that your sales team members educate your customers about these products/services as they serve them. Most business owners mistakenly assume their customers know about everything they sell. The fact is, customers are usually aware of less than one quarter of everything they sell.

- When selling a product that needs regular maintenance, you should sell service contracts as an optional extra. This ensures that customers will have all servicing of their products done by you. Arrange this at the time of purchase for best results. Remember to offer one-, two-, and five-year contracts. This will make it likely that they'll take the one-year contract at the very least.

- An easy way to gain more wallet share is to sell extended warranties or insurance. When your customers make a purchase, ask them if they would like an extended warranty. Your customers may well jump at the chance to buy that extra peace of mind particularly on major purchases. This must be done at the time of sale. You'll have more chances of succeeding here if you make this a really special offer.

- Running in-store promotions on a regular basis not only creates interest in products or services people buy as add-ons, or on impulse, it's also a great way to increase your profits. In-store promotions can take the form of product demonstrations, competitions, or sports personalities live in the store. Different events such as Easter, Christmas, or your store's birthday can also be turned into interesting promotions.

- Flashing light specials are a fun way to add to your bottom line. Now obviously, to run flashing light specials you need a flashing light or siren, which is then set off to direct people to products that are on sale. The sale should only last for 10–30 minutes. It's best to use flashing light specials when you have stock you wish to clear, damaged goods, or a new product.

Part 4

▮ Merchandise

"OK, Charlie, so far we've discussed some really powerful ways to bump up your profits. We've looked at three of the 4 Ms of Profit—Management, Money, and Marketing. That leaves just one, and that's Merchandise."

He stood up to stretch his legs, looked over to me, and said: "You mean stock?"

"Yes, that's exactly right. And it's a fascinating area, too."

"What can we do from a merchandise point of view to influence profit, Brad? Surely the manufacturers bind us? Unless we manufacture our own product, I suppose."

There's nothing I like better than a proactive student. You see, it's vitally important for people to participate when learning because that way they get to understand a lot more easily. And it sticks.

"Not so, Charlie. There's actually a whole lot you can do to directly influence your profit from a merchandise point of view. Let me give you an example."

I knew Charlie loves examples, especially if they are real-life ones. And I also know he's just like most people—being able to relate to something makes it a whole lot easier to grasp.

"In Blacktown, New South Wales, there's this firm called First Choice Protective Coating. It's owned by two brothers—Scott and John Paterson. It's a graffiti removal business. Now the Paterson brothers came into this business from different routes—Scott from the world of optics and John from plumbing. Both could be regarded as fairly typical tradespeople, and neither had any real business expertise to speak of. They did, however, have something going for them: They were enthusiastic, dedicated, and hard-working. And they happened to stumble across a product they believed could sell well."

So far so good. A fairly typical beginning. Thousands of business owners can tell a similar story.

"John's background was plumbing. He'd been a plumber all his life. He then moved into the wholesale side of the business and started a company that sold bathroom vanities, toilets, faucets, and that sort of thing. He spent his time wholesaling plumbing supplies to hardware stores.

"Then one day a Chemist said to him, 'when you're out selling your plumbing products to hardware stores, can you see if you can sell my graffiti removal products to them as well?' Well, he liked the idea and took it on, but nothing came of it initially."

Charlie was listening intently now. I had introduced the 4th M to the story— the merchandise. Now it was time to explain how this product came to change the fortunes of the company.

"They began taking a closer look at the graffiti product and decided it was worth spending time and effort trying to introduce it to the market. They began by selling three products: a Graffiti Remover liquid spray, a Graffiti Remover in gel form and a Sacrificial Antigraffiti Protective Coating."

"They then made up a few labels and began promoting the products to hardware stores and local councils. People were amazed, as they had never really heard of antigraffiti products before."

"It started selling; hardware stores began putting it on their shelves and it was proving quite a success for them. The only problem was, people were buying it but not reordering, so the brothers wanted to find out why."

"They then started putting their phone number on the labels. This generated calls from people asking them to remove graffiti for them, as they still weren't sure how to do it for themselves. Now this may come as something of a surprise. The brothers also had no experience in removing graffiti!"

"But once people started asking them to remove their graffiti, they thought they might as well give it a go. A new market was developing and they owed it to themselves to see whether it was something they could develop. After all, it could turn out to be quite profitable, they reasoned. So they bought a little pressure cleaner and thought they could make decent money by providing a service and selling the products at the same time."

"The ball started rolling and they began receiving more and more phone calls from clients."

I then told Charlie that the inevitable happened: Their business reached a plateau and the owners didn't know how to take it further."

"They contacted one of my Business Coaches, Greg. This worked wonders, and after a while the business blossomed. Turnover increased by 300 percent with profits rocketing up by 600 percent. The brothers are now looking at franchising the business. So, there you have it—a great example of how a business took a product, turned it into something exclusive, ran with it, and in so doing, transformed their business."

Charlie leaned back in his chair, exhaled loudly while running his fingers through his hair, then said, "That's amazing, Brad. But it couldn't happen to me. I mean—look at my business. What product could I possibly do the same with?"

"Don't be so negative, Charlie," I retorted. "You need to think laterally—and big. But you're jumping ahead now. Selling something on an exclusive basis is just one merchandise-related strategy that I'm going to discuss. There are many more, and you might find some of these will be perfect for you."

"Sorry, I suppose I'm just getting itchy to hear more. My mind keeps racing ahead, if you know what I mean."

"No worries. This is exciting stuff, believe me. But it's even more exciting when you see your bank account balance growing! It's now time to get into specifics."

What Are Merchandise-Related Strategies?

The very reason for being in business is to make a profit and the only way of achieving this is to provide customers, clients, consumers, or users with some type of product or service that they want—one that fills a specific need. And it's these products or services that I refer to here as merchandise. I use the word in the broadest sense, of course.

So, what then are merchandise-related strategies that are designed to have an influence on a company's bottom line? Am I referring to your stock per se? Will this section of the book zero in on what products or services will produce more profit for your business? Will you discover some sort of "insider tip" regarding what products to stock and which to avoid?

No, what I'm talking about in this chapter are those decisions management takes that concern the type of product lineup they stock, the strategies involving stock (in broad terms) that will lead directly to a healthier bottom line. I'm talking about the overall view management has of that area of a business that is concerned about the merchandise the business deals in, produces, or offers to its customers.

We're taking an umbrella view here—a macro view—looking from the top down, as it were. And it's fascinating what can be achieved simply by focusing your attention, as a business owner or manager, on your stock in trade. It may even reveal aspects of your business you never knew about. And once you begin taking a closer view of the merchandise-related facets of your business, new opportunities may well present themselves. New doors will begin to open. Evaluate them carefully, keeping profit firmly in mind. You may find your business heading in a whole new direction!

OK, so what does the word "merchandise" mean? According to the dictionary, it means "goods bought and sold in business." The word is derived from the Old French word *marchandise,* which meant "trade." The word merchant means, "One whose occupation is the wholesale purchase and retail sale of goods for profit." Isn't that interesting?

The Strategies

Sell More Big Margin Goods or Services

Because we are talking about management-related strategies here, this is a good one to start with. Make a decision to sell in the future only items that have a high margin built in.

This doesn't necessarily mean you should stock only expensive or exclusive up-market items. You see, quite often a lower-priced item will offer a greater margin. You should consider exactly how much each item makes you, and then continue to stock only those that make you the most money. If you work in the service industry, you should be considering which services offer the most money for the least amount of effort.

Take mechanical workshops, for instance. In the old days, they would almost certainly have sold fuel to their customers, but today, because there is very little margin in the price of fuel, many have opted instead to concentrate on mechanical servicing and repair work only, as the margins are far greater. They might not enjoy the same volume of business, but the profits are invariably higher.

If this strategy appeals to you, then before you start making decisions, you need to know exactly what the current margins are on everything you do or sell. Unless you know this, how will you be able to make an intelligent decision? How will you know if your business will be better or worse off? But if you have been working your way steadily (and diligently) through this book, that won't be an issue, will it? You'll already have a very good idea of what your margins are, as you will have already carried out a margin survey. But in case you haven't, now's the time to do it.

Once you know the margins on all of your products or services, select those high-margin ones that sell well. Then concentrate on them. Make them the flagships of your product lineup—your specialty. Isolate those items that offer the least margin and think very hard about whether it is really worth your while continuing to push them. Do they in fact cost you money when all is said and done? Could you not instead bundle them with your high-margin products as a way of adding perceived value? Could you not replace them with similar products that have better margins?

Stock More High-Priced Lines

It may sound obvious, but if you want to increase the profit you make from the product you sell, then sell more product that carries a higher price tag. You see, generally, the more an item sells for, the more profit you'll make. Now don't immediately assume this means a larger profit in percentage terms—it needn't. But it certainly means more profit in dollar terms. The percentage profit you make might be quite small, say 1 percent on a $300,000 service contract. That's $3000. But if you made a profit of 5 percent on a $10,000 service contract, that would only see $500 being tipped into your bank account.

There's another great strategic reason you should stock more high-priced lines than you currently do. You see, it gives you more flexibility on the sales floor. It gives you the chance to up-sell from your existing budget range. Have something to sell to those with more money to spend.

It also gives you the option of down-selling if the customer comes in to look at the more expensive item but decides against it. Once you've started stocking a higher-priced line, you may find that it receives complete customer acceptance. Then, once you've seen what this does to your bottom line, you might very well decide to drop the cheaper line altogether sometime in the future. If you do, care should be taken as this may result in your inadvertently changing your target market, something that can sometimes backfire.

Only Sell Fast-Moving Stock

I must point out here that it might not be possible for you to concentrate on high-margin products only. I'm sure every businessperson would love to, but factors outside their control might prevent this.

For instance, you might be part of an industry in which all products or services might be low in margin. Try selling new cars for anything approaching a decent margin. Or selling gasoline through a service station. In industries like these, profit is usually derived through the sheer volume of business they do instead.

This is why some service stations are quite happy not to offer mechanical repair and servicing facilities to their customers—their businesses generate sufficient revenue through high-volume fuel sales.

There's another good reason for selling only fast-moving stock, and it's this: Any stock that sits on shelves is wasting money. It's also tying up your capital, which could be put to better use buying more stock or earning interest in the bank. Furthermore, the longer it sits there on your shelves, the lower the margin you make on it when it finally goes. If the stock is particularly slow moving, it will probably need to be sold at a discounted price later on, costing you even more. So make sure that you stock only goods that move quickly.

My golden rule is to keep tabs on the turnover of each item or product you stock; if it's a fast mover, promote it even more, but if it's a slow mover, then dump it, or package it with higher-margin items to add value.

Carry Exclusive Lines

By stocking items that can't be purchased anywhere else, you can charge higher than normal prices. The advantage is that your customers can't shop around and get cheaper quotes. This is a great way to avoid "C"- and "D"-Grade customers, who'll continually ask for a discount.

Carrying exclusive lines has another advantage: It gives your business an air of exclusivity. It makes your business special. It makes it stand out.

When you are the only supplier or stockperson of a particular item, you become known as the expert on that product. This is great from a marketing point of view, as it's something you can push in your advertising. It also justifies your higher prices. And remember, people like buying from "experts." It gives them confidence that their buying decision was correct and that there's little chance that what they've been recommended by the salesperson as a solution is the best recommendation they could receive. It helps reduce their level of post-purchase trauma.

So, how do you get exclusive lines? Here are some ways:

- Ask your supplier. You may be able to get an exclusive arrangement, particularly if you're dealing with an overseas supplier and you are well entrenched in the local market. This is another good option if the product is new and the supplier hasn't yet had the opportunity to establish a distribution network.

- Repackage the product as your own. Very often manufacturers don't mind if you repackage their product as your own, giving it a different name and image. They are usually interested only in keeping their factory running and production lines rolling. They may even offer to do the rebranding for you. This is commonly done with so-called "no-name brands" at leading supermarket chains. They may even be willing to build in points of differentiation so that your product will be distinctly different from their run-of-the-mill product. Again, this is common practice in the motor industry where one manufacturer rebadges a model, giving it a different name and supplying it to a competitor to sell. But be careful, as repackaging can consume much of your profit.

Constantly shop around for the best deals, and continually ask your customers what they want, what their views are regarding your packaging, and what types and sizes they prefer. My overall message here is that by repackaging a product so that it carries your own label, you can greatly increase your margins on each product you sell.

- Manufacture your own. Depending on what it is you sell, it might be feasible to begin making your own product. If you're selling a lot of a particular item, you should look into the possibility of manufacturing it yourself. Obviously the benefit of making it yourself is that you get to keep the maximum amount of profit possible from each sale. Instead of your manufacturer making a lot and your making a bit, you get both slices. This strategy is one well worth looking into. But before you do, make sure you know everything about the manufacturing process. Budget very carefully and do the numbers. And don't discount the possibility of selling the product you now manufacture to your competitors. This could very well turn into the mainstay of your business!

- Hunt for a new product in an overseas market. Look for something that isn't yet available in your local market and negotiate with its supplier/manufacturer for an exclusive agency.

- Buy out your competition. Don't laugh—this has been done more than once before. Companies have bought out a competing company, only to close it down, simply to gain market share for their own product. Similarly, companies have taken over others just to gain control of their products. And depending on the industry you're operating in, this option can be cheaper than you'd imagine.

Sell Your Own Label

This is guaranteed to increase your slice of the profits. Selling your own label gives you the chance to discount certain lines to undercut your opposition. The beauty of this is that because there's no middleman, you're probably still making more profit than your opposition would be at full price.

Your own label also gives you exclusivity and the freedom to position it in the market wherever you want to. You won't have to follow the market and be cornered into a position where you have to accept a particular margin range just to stay competitive.

Marketing becomes easier, as you'll be able to stand out from the crowd and be noticed. Suddenly you'll have all sorts of marketing possibilities available to you that you might not have had before.

Sell Only Quality

Closely related to selling exclusive lines is selling quality products. If you restrict your product lineup to only the best, you'll be able to charge premium prices and benefit from better margins. Best of all you won't need to worry about customers bringing them back to be repaired. When considering the move to higher-quality stock, you need to keep two points in mind. First, the goods still have to be affordable for your existing clients. And secondly, you must be making more money from them per sale.

Make sure that the higher the price you charge, the higher the margin you make. Make quality your key selling point. Build it into your scripts and train your salespeople to emphasize constantly the advantages of quality over price. And one more thing: if you're selling only quality products, your service needs to match. Don't let sloppy customer service let you down.

Create a Quality Image

Present your store and your team members as professional and up-market. This will eliminate the bargain hunters to a large extent and will allow you to stock more expensive and profitable goods. Both your store and your team need to look immaculate at all times. You see, when customers walk into a store that has a quality image, they expect to receive quality service while they buy quality goods. And in exchange, they also expect to be charged quality prices. It goes with the territory.

So make sure that your team members dress well and reward those who are always impeccably presented. You may want to consider supplying them with a uniform. And don't overlook your premises. They must be clean, tidy, and well presented at all times.

Understand that image is more than skin deep. Image *is* reality. What your customers see and experience determines what they think about you. It determines their perception of you and your business. It's all they've got to go on initially, until they begin dealing with you and adding real-time information to their initial perception.

So don't allow either of these two factors to let you down. It's no use creating a great image, only to have it torn to shreds by shoddy service or inferior products. The two go hand-in-hand.

So make their shopping experience memorable. Doing so will also make it profitable for you.

What Else?

There are all sorts of other merchandise-related strategies you might want to consider to help get your profit graph track skywards. Some will be of a more strategic nature while others could even be considered "logical." But the point is, they work. Try one at a time, and then add to them as the results become apparent. You'll love the cumulative effect they'll have on your bottom line.

And remember to test and measure absolutely everything as you go along. That way you'll know what's working and what's not. But more about this in the next chapter.

So what are the other profit-boosting strategies? Here are my suggestions:

- Reduce your product line. You see, the longer an item sits on your shelf, the less profit you will eventually make from it. If you eliminate your slow-moving stock and only carry those lines which sell quickly you can make more money per item sold. Remember, the greater the range, the more suppliers you have accounts with, the more shelf space you need, the more money you have invested in stocks, the more costs you'll have, and so on.

- Take stock on consignment. This way you don't have to outlay money on stock that could take some time to move. You don't have to pay for it until it sells, which means your money can be working for you elsewhere. This is one of the most effective ways to increase your margins, and your profit.

- Reduce the amount of money you have tied up in inventory. Simple as it may seem, you should never have too much stock on hand, as it has an adverse affect on your cashflow. What's more, you run the risk of being stuck with it if trends change. Always keep your inventory as low as possible, without running short, and then only order as you need it.

- Buy in bulk, but only have your stock delivered in smaller shipments each month. This is a great idea if you've got smaller items that move quickly. The beauty of this strategy is that you only pay for each shipment as it arrives, yet you get it at the bulk price. This way you don't have to fork out for the whole lot in one hit, allowing you to invest the money elsewhere. Be sure to get a commitment from the supplier that the price won't rise along the way. Also establish that if the products don't arrive on time each month, you are entitled to some form of discount. You can also use this technique when selling to your customers, except this time focus on getting a commitment that forces them to pay for what's ordered at the designated times.

- Buy only what you need, because having an excess of stock reduces your company's cashflow. You should only carry a minimum amount of stock and then order more when you start to run low. You should also keep everyday costs down by only buying things like stationery if they're absolutely essential. And be absolutely ruthless about this! The key is to plan ahead so you never run out and have to resort to buying from the local store at three times the price. That would defeat the whole object of this exercise.

- Wherever possible, cut out the middlemen and buy direct from the manufacturer. This will save you a bundle. Another benefit is that it allows you to develop a working relationship with the manufacturer, which could lead to other great profit-boosting opportunities such as exclusive distribution rights, rebranding as your own label, or their making an exclusive product just for you.

- Sell off old stock. It's not making you any money sitting in a storeroom, and if it's on a shelf, then it's taking up space that could be occupied by a more profitable item. Selling off your old stock at cost or above creates extra revenue and allows you to display faster-moving goods with greater margins.

- Rearrange the layout of your store. How does this help increase your profit? It's all about presentation. You see, fast-moving items should be placed on or just above eye level with slow-moving items placed just below eye level. End aisle displays should tell a story with add-on sale items clearly visible. And make sure your most expensive items, or items with the highest margins, are in your highest-traffic areas. Make sure too that your products are on shelving that is clearly marked with bin labels. Not only will this assist your customers when purchasing, but it will also help you when reordering stock. A golden rule is that stock should be presented clearly with no broken packaging.

- Pay attention, too, to your point-of-sale material, as this assists in increasing your average dollar sale. These take the form of shelf talkers and bin labels and are available from your suppliers. If your current supplier isn't providing you with these "silent sales people," then call and request that they do. If you're making up your own point-of-sale signs, remember to focus on the benefits of the product. Including a list of accessories that are commonly purchased with that item can help boost sales. For example, if you've got a special on ravioli, it's vital you mention what sauces are available.

▌Testing and Measuring

Now that you've read through the sections on the various profit-building strategies, you're probably itching to implement a few right away. And why not—there's no time like *now* to take control of your business, your future, and your destiny.

But before you do, there's just one more concept we need to expand upon, and that's testing and measuring.

If you're not testing and measuring everything you do, you also won't know what's working and what's not. You won't know which strategies to keep going, which to drop, and which to give more time to because they're showing promising signs.

This means you should be doing two things when implementing profit-boosting strategies: You need to conduct two surveys to determine exactly what your average dollar sale is and what your average margins are *before* the strategies are implemented, and you need to test and measure the results of your strategies *as you go along*. That way you can refine, hone, fine tune, redirect, or cancel strategies before they cost you lots of money and have the opposite effect than that which you originally wanted—more profit.

So let's work through these.

The first thing you need to do is determine where your business is at present, profitwise. You need to find out what your average dollar sale is and what margins you're making. To do this you need to conduct a survey—well, two actually: one to determine just what your average dollar sale is, and the other to get a handle on what your margins are. This was discussed earlier in this book, but if you didn't do it then, *do it now*.

Decide which of the powerful profit-building strategies directly applies to your business. There probably is a lot, but start off by choosing just a few. It doesn't matter which ones they are, but it makes sense to choose one from each of the major areas to begin with. That way it will be easier for you to test and measure.

Here's what to do from here on in:

Step 1

Once you've set in place arrangements to implement your chosen strategies, redesign the *Testing and Measuring Sheets* to monitor their results.

Let's look at the *Average Dollar Sale Testing and Measuring Sheet* first. Yours should look something like this:

AVERAGE DOLLAR SALE SURVEY

Date: _____

Salesperson: _____

CUSTOMER #   DOLLARS SPENT

_____   _____

_____   _____

_____   _____

_____   _____

_____   _____

_____   _____

_____   _____

DAILY SUMMARY

No. of Customers: _____

Total Dollars Spent: _____

Average Dollar Sale for the Day: _____
(Total Dollars ÷ No. of Customers)

Let's now look at your Margins Testing and Measuring Sheet.

Once again, adapt the sheet as required. It should look something like this:

MARGIN SURVEY

Date: _____

Department or Product Line	Item	Margin
_____	_____	_____
	_____	_____
	_____	_____
_____	_____	_____
	_____	_____
	_____	_____
_____	_____	_____
	_____	_____
	_____	_____
_____	_____	_____
	_____	_____

Obviously the survey form you use should be designed to reflect the type of business you're in.

Step 2

Prune, modify, and increase. Identify which of your chosen strategies are working and which aren't. Scale back strategies that seem excessive, modify those that may produce slightly better results with a bit of tweaking, and increase those that are working well.

Step 3

Test and measure for another two weeks. Use fresh survey forms. Notice what is happening to your results. Are your Average Dollar Sale and Margin figures going up, down, or staying the same?

Step 4

Check your strategies. Be honest with yourself. Are you cutting corners or being diligent? And what about the rest of your team members? Have they been fully briefed and do they understand the reasons for doing what they're doing? Have you implemented the strategies correctly? Are you recording the results properly?

Step 5

Consolidate. Leave things as they are now for a month or so and work on your customers; convert new leads into customers, and then get them to visit again. You want them to become repeat customers.

Step 6

Branch out. Now's the time to implement some of the other new strategies you'll have chosen but didn't implement at first. Do one at a time and track the results meticulously by repeating Steps 3 to 5 above. Compare the results you get with those you determined through your initial surveys conducted right at the beginning, before you started implementing the profit-building strategies.

If you're not getting the results you want, try the next strategy selected from the vast number mentioned in this book. But don't be disheartened—you may need to try a few before you reach the results you're after. You see, every industry is different: What works well for one might not work for another. Some businesses may not deal directly with the buying public, making certain strategies irrelevant (although most can be adapted to suit any situation).

You may find that more than one strategy needs to be implemented simultaneously. That's fine. Very often, five or six profit-increasing strategies together produce a compound effect that sends the bottom line rocketing.

But don't flog a dead horse just because you happen to *like* one particular strategy or because you think it *should* work. If at first it doesn't work, give it another try, then another. But after that, if you still see negative (or inconclusive) results, then drop it.

∎ Conclusion

So there you have it—everything you need to know to improve your bottom line.

Profit-building strategies serve a number of very important purposes in business. First, they focus your mind and attention on what needs to be done to maximize your profits by increasing your average dollar sale and maximizing your margins. Secondly, by throwing the spotlight on these two areas, you could learn things about your business you never knew before.

Once you've worked your way through this book, you'll know what the 4 Ms of Profit are. You'll also know precisely what strategies to use to maximize the financial results achieved from each of these areas.

But that's not all. You will, perhaps for the first time, know how much money your customers spend, on average. And you'll have a very accurate picture of your margins. These may have come as something of a revelation to you; many business owners are quite taken aback on discovering these figures for the first time. They find them nothing short of embarrassing, shocking, or even disgraceful. What about you? What were you're first feelings after completing the two surveys?

So, if you fit into this category, don't despair. Just think how sweet it will feel once you've been able to drastically alter these results.

By the time you've worked your way though this book, you'll also know the true value of testing and measuring. You'll have seen the value of incorporating it into your daily routine. And you'll also be able to accurately analyze the costs of implementing the various strategies chosen.

So what are you waiting for? It's time to get into *Action*.

▌Getting into *Action*

So, when is the best time to start?

Now—right now—so let me give you a step-by-step method to get yourself onto the same success path of many of my clients and the clients of my team at *Action International*.

Start testing and measuring now.

You'll want to ask your customers and prospects how they found out about you and your business. This will give you an idea of what's been working and what hasn't. You also want to concentrate on the five areas of the business chassis. Remember:

1. Number of Leads from each campaign.
2. Conversion Rate from each and every campaign.
3. Number of Transactions on average per year per customer.
4. Average Dollar Sale from each campaign.
5. Your Margins on each product or service.

The Number of Leads is easy; just take a measure for four weeks, average it out, and multiply by 50 working weeks of the year. Of course you'd ask each lead where they came from so you've got enough information to make advertising decisions.

The Conversion Rate is a little trickier, not because it's hard to measure, but because we want to know a few more details. You want to know what level of conversion you have from each and every type of marketing strategy you use. Remember that some customers won't buy right away, so keep accurate records on each and every lead.

To find the Number of Transactions you'll need to go through your records. Hopefully you can find the transaction history of at least 50 of your past customers and then average out their yearly purchases.

The Average Dollar Sale is as simple as it sounds. The total dollars sold divided by the number of sales. The best information you can collect is the average from each marketing campaign you run, so that you know where the real profit is coming from.

And, of course, your margins. An Average Margin is good to know and measure, but to know the margins on everything you sell is the most powerful knowledge you can collect.

If you're having any challenges with your testing and measuring, be sure to contact your nearest *Action International* Business Coach. She'll be able to help you through and show you the specialized documents to use.

If, by chance, you're thinking of racing ahead before you test and measure, remember this. It's impossible to improve a score when you don't know what the score is.

So you've got your starting point. You know exactly what's going on in your business right now. In fact, you know more about not only what's happening right now, but also the factors that are going to create what will happen tomorrow.

The next step in your business growth is simple.

Let's decide what you want out of the business—in other words, your goals. Here are the main points I want you to plan for.

How many hours do you want to work each week? How much money do you want to take out of the business each month? And, most importantly, when do you want to finish the business?

By "finish" the business, I mean when it will be systematized enough so it can run without your having to be there. Remember this about business; a little bit of planning goes a long way, but to make a plan you have to have a destination.

Once again, if you're having difficulty, talk to an *Action International* Business Coach. He'll know exactly how to help you find what it is you really want out of both your business and your life.

Now the real work begins.

Remember, our goal is to get a 10 percent increase in each area over the next 12 months. Choose well, but I want to warn you of one thing, one thing I can literally guarantee.

Eight out of 10 marketing campaigns you run *will not work.*

That's why when you choose to run, say, an advertising campaign in your local newspaper, you've got to run at least 10 different ads. When you select a direct mail campaign, you should send out at least 10 different letters to test, and so on.

Make sure you get at least five strategies under each heading and plan to run at least one, preferably two, at least each month for the next 12 months.

Don't work on just one of the five areas at a time; mix it up a little so you get the synergy of all five areas working together.

Now, this is the most important advice I can give you:

Learn how to make each and every strategy work. Don't just think you know what to do; go through my hints and tips, read more books, listen to as many tapes as you can, watch all the videos you can find, talk to the experts, and make sure you get the most advantage you can before you invest a whole lot of money.

The next 12 months are going to be a matter of doing the numbers, running the campaigns, testing headlines, testing offers, testing prices, and, of course, measuring the results.

By the end of it you should have at least five new strategies in each of the five areas working together to produce a great result.

Once again I want to stress that this will work and this will make your business grow as long as *you* work it.

Is it simple? *Yes.*

Is it easy? *No.*

You'll have to work hard. If you can get the guidance of someone who's been there before you, then get it.

Whatever you do, start it now, start it today, and most importantly, make the most of every day. Your past does not equal your future; you decide your future right here and right now.

Be who you want to be, *do* what you need to do, in order to *have* what you want to have.

Positive *thought* without positive *Action* leaves you with positively *nothing.* I called my company *Action International,* not Theory International, or Yeah, I read that book International, but *Action International.*

So take the first step—and get into *Action.*

■ ABOUT THE AUTHOR

Bradley J. Sugars

Brad Sugars is a world-renowned Australian entrepreneur, author, and business coach who has helped more than a million clients around the world find business and personal success.

He's a trained accountant, but as he puts it, most of his experience comes from owning his own companies. Brad's been in business for himself since age 15 in some way or another, although his father would argue he started at 7 when he was caught selling his Christmas presents to his brothers. He's owned and operated more than two dozen companies, from pizza to ladies fashion, from real estate to insurance and many more.

His main company, *Action International,* started from humble beginnings in the back bedroom of a suburban home in 1993 when Brad started teaching business owners how to grow their sales and marketing results. Now *Action* has nearly 1000 franchises in 19 countries and is ranked in the top 100 franchises in the world.

Brad Sugars has spoken on stage with the likes of Tom Hopkins, Brian Tracy, John Maxwell, Robert Kiyosaki, and Allen Pease, written books with people like Anthony Robbins, Jim Rohn, and Mark Victor Hansen, appeared on countless TV and radio programs and in literally hundreds of print articles around the globe. He's been voted as one of the Most Admired Entrepreneurs by the readers of *E-Spy* magazine—next to the likes of Rupert Murdoch, Henry Ford, Richard Branson, and Anita Roddick.

Today, *Action International* has coaches across the globe and is ranked as one of the Top 25 Fastest Growing Franchises on the planet as well as the #1 Business Consulting Franchise. The success of *Action International* is simply attributed to the fact that they apply the strategies their coaches use with business owners.

Brad is a proud father and husband, the chairman of a major children's charity, and in his own words, "a very average golfer."

Check out Brad's Web site www.bradsugars.com and read the literally hundreds of testimonials from those who've gone before you.

■ RECOMMENDED READING LIST

ACTION INTERNATIONAL BOOK LIST

"The only difference between *you* now and *you* in 5 years' time will be the people you meet and the books you read." Charlie Tremendous Jones

"And, the only difference between *your* income now and *your* income in 5 years' time will be the people you meet, the books you read, the tapes you listen to, and then how *you* apply it all." Brad Sugars

- *The E-Myth Revisited* by Michael E. Gerber
- *My Life in Advertising & Scientific Advertising* by Claude Hopkins
- *Tested Advertising Methods* by John Caples
- *Building the Happiness Centered Business* by Dr. Paddi Lund
- *Write Language* by Paul Dunn & Alan Pease
- *7 Habits of Highly Effective People* by Steven Covey
- *First Things First* by Steven Covey
- *Awaken the Giant Within* by Anthony Robbins
- *Unlimited Power* by Anthony Robbins
- *22 Immutable Laws of Marketing* by Al Ries & Jack Trout
- *21 Ways to Build a Referral Based Business* by Brad Sugars
- *21 Ways to Increase Your Advertising Response* by Mark Tier
- *The One Minute Salesperson* by Spencer Johnson & Larry Wilson
- *The One Minute Manager* by Spencer Johnson & Kenneth Blanchard
- *The Great Sales Book* by Jack Collis
- *Way of the Peaceful Warrior* by Dan Millman
- *How to Build a Championship Team*—Six Audio tapes by Blair Singer
- Brad Sugars "Introduction to Sales & Marketing" 3-hour Video
- Leverage—Board Game by Brad Sugars
- *17 Ways to Increase Your Business Profits* booklet & tape by Brad Sugars. FREE OF CHARGE to Business Owners

*To order Brad Sugars' products from the recommended reading list, call your nearest *Action International* office today.

The 18 Most Asked Questions about Working with an *Action International* Business Coach

And 18 great reasons why you'll jump at the chance to get your business flying and make your dreams come true

1. So who is *Action International?*

Action International is a business Coaching and Consulting company started in 1993 by entrepreneur and author Brad Sugars. With offices around the globe and business coaches from Singapore to Sydney to San Francisco, *Action International* has been set up with you, the business owner, in mind.

Unlike traditional consulting firms, *Action* is designed to give you both short-term assistance and long-term training through its affordable Mentoring approach. After 12 years teaching business owners how to succeed, *Action's* more than 10,000 clients and 1,000,000 seminar attendees will attest to the power of the programs.

Based on the sales, marketing, and business management systems created by Brad Sugars, your *Action* Coach is trained to not only show you how to increase your business revenues and profits, but also how to develop the business so that you as the owner work less and relax more.

Action International is a franchised company, so your local *Action* Coach is a fellow business owner who's invested her own time, money, and energy to make her business succeed. At *Action,* your success truly does determine our success.

2. And, why do I need a Business Coach?

Every great sports star, business person, and superstar is surrounded by coaches and advisors.

And, as the world of business moves faster and gets more competitive, it's difficult to keep up with both the changes in your industry and the innovations in sales, marketing, and management strategies. Having a business coach is no longer a luxury; it's become a necessity.

On top of all that, it's impossible to get an objective answer from yourself. Don't get me wrong. You can survive in business without the help of a Coach, but it's almost impossible to thrive.

A Coach *can* see the forest for the trees. A Coach will make you focus on the game. A Coach will make you run more laps than you feel like. A Coach will tell it like it is. A Coach will give you small pointers. A Coach will listen. A Coach will be your marketing manager, your sales director, your training coordinator, your partner, your confidant, your mentor, your best friend, and an *Action* Business Coach will help you make your dreams come true.

3. Then, what's an Alignment Consultation?

Great question. It's where an *Action* Coach starts with every business owner. You'll invest a minimum of $1295, and during the initial 2 to 3 hours your Coach invests with you, he'll learn as much as he can about your business, your goals, your challenges, your sales, your marketing, your finances, and so much more.

All with three goals in mind: To know exactly where your business is now. To clarify your goals both in the business and personally. And thirdly, to get the crucial pieces of information he needs to create your businesses *Action* Plan for the next 12 months.

Not a traditional business or marketing plan mind you, but a step-by-step plan of *Action* that you'll work through as you continue with the Mentor Program.

4. So, what, then, is the Mentor Program?

Simply put, it's where your *Action* Coach will work with you for a full 12 months to make your goals a reality. From weekly coaching calls and goal-setting sessions, to creating marketing pieces together, you will develop new sales strategies and business systems so you can work less and learn all that you need to know about how to make your dreams come true.

You'll invest between $995 and $10,000 a month and your Coach will dedicate a minimum of 5 hours a month to working with you on your sales, marketing, team building, business development, and every step of the *Action* Plan you created from your Alignment Consultation.

Unlike most consultants, your *Action* Coach will do more than just show you what to do. She'll be with you when you need her most, as each idea takes shape, as each campaign is put into place, as you need the little pointers on making it happen, when you need someone to talk to, when you're faced with challenges and, most importantly, when you're just not sure what to do next. Your Coach will be there every step of the way.

5. Why at least 12 months?

If you've been in business for more than a few weeks, you've seen at least one or two so called "quick fixes."

Most Consultants seem to think they can solve all your problems in a few hours or a few days. At *Action* we believe that long-term success means not just scraping the surface and doing it for you. It means doing it with you, showing you how to do it, working alongside you, and creating the success together.

Over the 12 months, you'll work on different areas of your business, and month by month you'll not only see your goals become a reality, you'll gain both the confidence and the knowledge to make it happen again and again, even when your first 12 months of Coaching is over.

6. How can you be sure this will work in my industry and in my business?

Very simple. You see at *Action,* we're experts in the areas of sales, marketing, business development, business management, and team building just to name a few. With 328 different profit-building strategies, you'll soon see just how powerful these systems are.

You, on the other hand, are the expert in your business and together we can apply the *Action* systems to make your business fly.

Add to this the fact that within the *Action* Team at least one of our Coaches has either worked with, managed, worked in, or even owned a business that's the same or very similar to yours. Your *Action* Coach has the full resources of the entire *Action* team to call upon for every challenge you have. Imagine hundreds of experts ready to help you.

7. Won't this just mean more work?

Of course when you set the plan with your *Action* Coach, it'll all seem like a massive amount of work, but no one ever said attaining your goals would be easy.

In the first few months, it'll take some work to adjust, some work to get over the hump so to speak. The further you are into the program, the less and less work you'll have to do.

You will, however, be literally amazed at how focused you'll be and how much you'll get done. With focus, an *Action* Coach, and most importantly the *Action* Systems, you'll be achieving a whole lot more with the same or even less work.

8. How will I find the time?

Once again the first few months will be the toughest, not because of an extra amount of work, but because of the different work. In fact, your *Action* Coach will show you how to, on a day-to-day basis, get more work done with less effort.

In other words, after the first few months you'll find that you're not working more, just working differently. Then, depending on your goals from about month six onwards, you'll start to see the results of all your work, and if you choose to, you can start working less than ever before. Just remember, it's about changing what you do with your time, *not* putting in more time.

9. How much will I need to invest?

Nothing, if you look at it from the same perspective as we do. That's the difference between a cost and an investment. Everything you do with your *Action* Coach is a true investment in your future.

Not only will you create great results in your business, but you'll end up with both an entrepreneurial education second to none, and the knowledge that you can repeat your successes over and over again.

As mentioned, you'll need to invest at least $1295 up to $5000 for the Alignment Consultation and Training Day, and then between $995 and $10,000 a month for the next 12 months of coaching.

Your Coach may also suggest several books, tapes, and videos to assist in your training, and yes, they'll add to your investment as you go. Why? Because having an *Action* Coach is just like having a marketing manager, a sales team leader, a trainer, a recruitment specialist, and corporate consultant all for half the price of a secretary.

10. Will it cost me extra to implement the strategies?

Once again, give your *Action* Coach just half an hour and he'll show you how to turn your marketing into an investment that yields sales and profits rather than just running up your expenses.

In most cases we'll actually save you money when we find the areas that aren't working for you. But yes, I'm sure you'll need to spend some money to make some money.

Yet, when you follow our simple testing and measuring systems, you'll never risk more than a few dollars on each campaign, and when we find the ones that work, we make sure you keep profiting from them time and again.

Remember, when you go the accounting way of saving costs, you can only ever add a few percent to the bottom line.

Following Brad Sugars' formula, your *Action* Coach will show you that through sales, marketing, and income growth, your possible returns are exponential.

The sky's the limit, as they say.

11. Are there any guarantees?

To put it bluntly, no. Your *Action* Coach will never promise any specific results, nor will she guarantee that any of your goals will become a reality.

You see, we're your coach. You're still the player, and it's up to you to take the field. Your Coach will push you, cajole you, help you, be there for you, and even do some things with you, but you've still got to do the work.

Only *you* can ever be truly accountable for your own success and at *Action* we know this to be a fact. We guarantee to give you the best service we can, to answer your questions promptly, and with the best available information. And, last but not least your *Action* Coach is committed to making you successful whether you like it or not.

That's right, once we've set the goals and made the plan, we'll do whatever it takes to make sure you reach for that goal and strive with all your might to achieve all that you desire.

Of course we'll be sure to keep you as balanced in your life as we can. We'll make sure you never compromise either the long-term health and success of your company or yourself, and more importantly your personal set of values and what's important to you.

12. What results have other business owners seen?

Anything from previously working 60 hours a week down to working just 10—right through to increases in revenues of 100s and even 1000s of percent. Results speak for themselves. Be sure to keep reading for specific examples of real people, with real businesses, getting real results.

There are three reasons why this will work for you in your business. Firstly, your *Action* Coach will help you get 100 percent focused on your goals and the step-by-step processes to get you there. This focus alone is amazing in its effect on you and your business results.

Secondly, your coach will hold you accountable to get things done, not just for the day-to-day running of the business, but for the dynamic growth of the business. You're investing in your success and we're going to get you there.

Thirdly, your Coach is going to teach you one-on-one as many of *Action's* 328 profit-building strategies as you need. So whether your goal is to be making more money, or working fewer hours or both inside the next 12 months your goals can become a reality. Just ask any of the thousands of existing *Action* clients, or more specifically, check out the results of 19 of our most recent clients shown later in this section.

13. What areas will you coach me in?

There are five main areas your *Action* Coach will work on with you. Of course, how much of each depends on you, your business, and your goals.

Sales. The backbone of creating a superprofitable business, and one area we'll help you get spectacular results in.

Marketing and Advertising. If you want to get a sale, you've got to get a prospect. Over the next 12 months your *Action* Coach will teach you Brad Sugars' amazingly simple streetwise marketing—marketing that makes profits.

Team Building and Recruitment. You'll never *wish* for the right people again. You'll have motivated and passionate team members when your Coach shows you how.

Systems and Business Development. Stop the business from running you and start running your business. Your Coach will show you the secrets to having the business work, even when you're not there.

Customer Service. How to deliver consistently, make it easy to buy, and leave your customers feeling delighted with your service. Both referrals and repeat business are centered in the strategies your Coach will teach you.

14. Can you also train my people?

Yes. We believe that training your people is almost as important as coaching you.

Your investment starts at $1500 for your entire team, and you can decide between five very powerful in-house training programs. From "*Sales Made Simple*" for your face-to-face sales team to "*Phone Power*" for your entire team's telephone etiquette and sales ability. Then you can run the *"Raving Fans"* customer service training or the *"Total Team"* training. And finally, if you're too busy earning a living to make any real money, then you've just got to attend our *"Business Academy 101."* It will make a huge impact on your finances, business, career, family, and lifestyle. You'll be amazed at how much involvement and excitement comes out of your team with each training program.

15. Can you write ads, letters, and marketing pieces for me?

Yes. Your *Action* Coach can do it for you, he can train you to do it yourself, or we can simply critique the marketing pieces you're using right now.

If you want us to do it for you, our one-time fees start at just $1195. You'll not only get one piece; we'll design several pieces for you to take to the market and see which one performs the best. Then, if it's a critique you're after, just $349 means we'll work through your entire piece and give you feedback on what to change, how to change it, and what else you should do. Last but not least, for between $15 and $795 we can recommend a variety of books, tapes, and most importantly, Brad Sugars' Instant Success series books that'll take you step-by-step through the how-tos of creating your marketing pieces.

16. Why do you also recommend books, tapes, and videos?

Basically, to save you time and money. Take Brad Sugars' *Sales Rich* DVD or Video Series, for instance. In about 16 hours you'll learn more about business than you have in the last 12 years. It'll also mean your *Action* Coach works with you on the high-level implementation rather than the very basic teaching.

It's a very powerful way for you to speed up the coaching process and get phenomenal rather than just great results.

17. When is the best time to get started?

Yesterday. OK, seriously, right now, today, this minute, before you take another step, waste another dollar, lose another sale, work too many more hours, miss another family event, forget another special occasion.

Far too many business people wait and see. They think working harder will make it all better. Remember, what you know got you to where you are. To get to where you want to go, you've got to make some changes and most probably learn something new.

There's no time like the present to get started on your dreams and goals.

18. So how do we get started?

Well, you'd better get back in touch with your *Action* Coach. There's some very simple paperwork to sign, and then you're on your way.

You'll have to invest a few hours showing them everything about your business. Together you'll get a plan created and then the work starts. Remember, it may seem like a big job at the start, but with a Coach, you're sharing the load and together you'll achieve great things.

Here's what others say about what happened after working with an *Action* business coach

Paul and Rosemary Rose—Icontact Multimedia

"Our *Action* coach showed us several ways to help market our product. We went on to triple our client base and simultaneously tripled our profits in just seven months. It was unbelievable! Last year was our best Christmas ever. We were really able to spoil ourselves!"

S. Ford—Pride Kitchens

"In 6 months, I've gone from working more than 60 hours per week in my business to less than 20, and my conversion rate's up from 19 percent to 62 percent. I've now got some life back!"

Gary and Leanne Paper—Galea Timber Products

"We achieved our goal for the 12 months within a 6-month period with a 100 percent increase in turnover and a good increase in margins. We have already recommended and will continue to recommend this program to others."

Russell, Kevin, John, and Karen—Northern Lights Power and Distribution

"Our profit margin has increased from 8 percent to 21 percent in the last 8 months. *Action* coaching focussed us on what are our most profitable markets."

Ty Pedersen—De Vries Marketing Sydney

"After just three months of coaching, my sales team's conversion rate has grown from an average of less than 12 percent to more than 23 percent and our profits have climbed by more than 30 percent."

Hank Meerkerk and Hemi McGarvey—B.O.P. School of Welding

"Last year we started off with a profit forecast, but as soon as we got *Action* involved we decided to double our forecast. We're already well over that forecast again by two-and-a-half times on turnover, and profits are even higher. Now we run a really profitable business."

Stuart Birch—Education Personnel Limited

"One direct mail letter added $40,000 to my bottom line, and working with *Action* has given me quality time to work on my business and spend time with my family."

Mark West—Wests Pumping and Irrigation

"In four months two simple strategies have increased our business more than 20 percent. We're so busy, we've had to delay expanding the business while we catch up!"

Michael Griffiths—Gym Owner

"I went from working 70 hours per week *in* the business to just 25 hours, with the rest of the time spent working *on* the business."

Cheryl Standring—In Harmony Landscapes

"We tried our own direct mail and only got a 1 percent response. With *Action* our response rate increased to 20 percent. It's definitely worth every dollar we've invested."

Jason and Chris Houston—Empradoor Finishing

"After 11 months of working with *Action,* we have increased our sales by 497 percent, and the team is working without our having to be there."

Michael Avery—Coomera Pet Motels

"I was skeptical at first, but I knew we needed major changes in our business. In 2 months, our extra profits were easily covering our investment and our predictions for the next 10 months are amazing."

Garry Norris—North Tax & Accounting

"As an accountant, my training enables me to help other business people make more money. It is therefore refreshing when someone else can help me do the same. I have a policy of only referring my clients to people who are professional, good at what they do, and who have personally given me great service. *Action* fits all three of these criteria, and I recommend *Action* to my business clients who want to grow and develop their businesses further."

Lisa Davis and Steve Groves—Mt. Eden Motorcycles

"With *Action* we increased our database from 800 to 1200 in 3 months. We consistently get about 20 new qualified people on our database each week for less than $10 per week."

Christine Pryor—U-Name-It Embroidery

"Sales for August this year have increased 352 percent. We're now targeting a different market and we're a lot more confident about what we're doing."

Joseph Saitta and Michelle Fisher—Banyule Electrics

"Working with *Action*, our inquiry rate has doubled. In four months our business has changed so much our customers love us. It's a better place for people to work and our margins are widening."

Kevin and Alison Snook—Property Sales

"In the 12 months previous to working with *Action*, we had sold one home in our subdivision. In the first eight months of working with *Action*, we sold six homes. The results speak for themselves."

Wayne Manson—Hospital Supplies

"When I first looked at the Mentoring Program it looked expensive, but from the inside looking out, its been the best money I have ever spent. Sales are up more than $3000 per month since I started, and the things I have learned and expect to learn will ensure that I will enjoy strong sustainable growth in the future."

■ *Action* Contact Details

Action International Asia Pacific

Ground Floor, *Action* House, 2 Mayneview Street, Milton QLD 4064

Ph: +61 (0) 7 3368 2525

Fax: +61 (0) 7 3368 2535

Free Call: 1800 670 335

Action International Europe

Olympic House, Harbor Road, Howth, Co. Dublin, Ireland

Ph: +353 (0) 1-8320213

Fax: +353 (0) 1-8394934

Action International North America

5670 Wynn Road Suite A & C, Las Vegas, Nevada 89118

Ph: +1 (702) 795 3188

Fax: +1 (702) 795 3183

Free Call: (888) 483 2828

Action International UK

3–5 Richmond Hill, Richmond, Surrey TW10 6RE

Ph: +44 020 8948 5151

Fax: +44 020 8948 4111

Action Offices around the globe:

Australia | Canada | China | England | France | Germany | Hong Kong

India | Indonesia | Ireland | Malaysia | Mexico | New Zealand

Phillippines | Scotland | Spain | Singapore | USA | Wales

Here's how you can profit from all of Brad's ideas with your local *Action* *International* Business Coach

Just like a sporting coach pushes an athlete to achieve optimum performance, provides them with support when they are exhausted, and teaches the athlete to execute plays that the competition does not anticipate.

A business coach will make you run more laps than you feel like. A business coach will show it like it is. And a business coach will listen.

The role of an *Action* Business Coach is to show you how to improve your business through guidance, support, and encouragement. Your coach will help you with your sales, marketing, management, team building, and so much more. Just like a sporting coach, your *Action* Business Coach will help you and your business perform at levels you never thought possible.

Whether you've been in business for a week or 20 years, it's the right time to meet with and see how you'll profit from an *Action* Coach.

As the owner of a business it's hard enough to keep pace with all the changes and innovations going on in your industry, let alone to find the time to devote to sales, marketing, systems, planning and team management, and then to run your business as well.

As the world of business moves faster and becomes more competitive, having a Business Coach is no longer a luxury; it has become a necessity. Based on the sales, marketing, and business management systems created by Brad Sugars, your *Action* Coach is trained to not only show you how to increase your business revenues and profits but also how to develop your business so that you, as the owner, can take back control. All with the aim of your working less and relaxing more. Making money is one thing; having the time to enjoy it is another.

Your *Action* Business Coach will become your marketing manager, your sales director, your training coordinator, your confidant, your mentor. In short, your *Action* Coach will help you make your business dreams come true.

ATTENTION BUSINESS OWNERS
You can increase your profits now

Here's how you can have one of Brad's *Action* International Business Coaches guide you to success.

Like every successful sporting icon or team, a business needs a coach to help it achieve its full potential. In order to guarantee your business success, you can have one of Brad's team as your business coach. You will learn about how you can get amazing results with the help of the team at *Action* International.

The business coaches are ready to take you and your business on a journey that will reward you for the rest of your life. You see, we believe *Action* speaks louder than words.

Complete and post this card to your local *Action* office to discover how our team can help you increase your income today!

Action International

The World's Number-1 Business Coaching Team

Name ....

Position ....

Company ....

Address ....

....

Country ....

Phone ....

Fax ....

Email ....

Referred by ....

How do I become an *Action* International **Business Coach?**

If you choose to invest your time and money in a great business and you're looking for a white-collar franchise opportunity to build yourself a lifestyle, an income, a way to take control of your life and, a way to get great personal satisfaction ...

Then you've just found the world's best team!

Now, it's about finding out if you've got what it takes to really enjoy and thrive in this amazing business opportunity.

Here are the 4 things we look for in every *Action* Coach:

1. You've got to love succeeding

We're looking for people who love success, who love getting out there and making things happen. People who enjoy mixing with other people, people who thrive on learning and growing, and people who want to charge an hourly rate most professionals only dream of.

2. You've got to love being in charge of your own life

When you're ready to take control, the key is to be in business for yourself, but not by yourself. *Action*'s support, our training, our world leading systems, and the backup of a global team are all waiting to give you the best chance of being an amazing business success.

3. You've got to love helping people

Being a great Coach is all about helping yourself by helping others. The first time clients thank you for showing them step by step how to make more money and work less within their business, will be the day you realize just how great being an *Action* Business Coach really is.

4. You've got to love a great lifestyle

Working from home, setting your own timetable, spending time with family and friends, knowing that the hard work you do is for your own company and, not having to climb a so-called corporate ladder. This is what lifestyle is all about. Remember, business is supposed to give you a life, not take it away.

Our business is booming and we're seriously looking for people ready to find out more about how becoming a member of the *Action* International Business Coaching team is going to be the best decision you've ever made.

Apply online now at www.action-international.com

Here's how you can network, get new leads, build yourself an instant sales team, learn, grow and build a great team of supportive business owners around you by checking into your local *Action* Profit Club

Joining your local *Action* Profit Club is about more than just networking, it's also the learning and exchanging of profitable ideas.

Embark on a journey to a more profitable enterprise by meeting with fellow, like-minded business owners.

An *Action* Profit Club is an excellent way to network with business people and business owners. You will meet every two weeks for breakfast to network and learn profitable strategies to grow your business.

Here are three reasons why *Action* *International's* Profit Clubs work where other networking groups don't:

1. You know networking is a great idea. The challenge is finding the time and maintaining the motivation to keep it up and make it a part of your business. If you're not really having fun and getting the benefits, you'll find it gets easier to find excuses that stop you going. So, we guarantee you will always have fun and learn a lot from your bi-weekly group meetings.
2. The real problem is that so few people do any work 'on' their business. Instead they generally work "in" it, until it's too late. By being a member of an *Action* Profit Club, you get to attend FREE business-building workshops run by Business Coaches that teach you how to work "on" your business and avoid this common pitfall and help you to grow your business.
3. Unlike other groups, we have marketing systems to assist in your groups' growth rather than just relying on you to bring in new members. This way you can concentrate on YOUR business rather than on ours.

Latest statistics show that the average person knows at least 200 other contacts. By being a member of your local *Action* Profit Club, you have an instant network of around 3,000 people

Join your local *Action* Profit Club today.

Apply online now at www.actionprofitclub.com

LEVERAGE—The Game of Business
Your Business Success is just a Few Games Away

Leverage—The Game of Business is a fun way to learn how to succeed in business fast.

The rewards start flowing the moment you start playing!

Leverage is three hours of fun, learning, and discovering how you can be an amazingly successful business person.

It's a breakthrough in education that will have you racking up the profits in no time. The principles you take away from playing this game will set you up for a life of business success. It will open your mind to what's truly possible. Apply what you learn and **sit back and watch your profits soar.**

By playing this fun and interactive business game, you will learn:

- How to quickly raise your business income
- How business people can become rich and successful in a short space of time
- How to create a business that works without you

Isn't it time you had the edge over your competition?

Leverage has been played by all age groups from 12-85 and has been a huge learning experience for all. The most common comment we hear is: 'I thought I knew a lot, and just by playing a simple board game I have realized I have a long way to go. The knowledge I've gained from playing Leverage will make me thousands! Thanks for the lesson.'

To order your copy online today, please visit www.bradsugars.com

Instant Success series.

INSTANT CASHFLOW
Turn every lead into a sale
(0-07-146659-2)

BILLIONAIRE IN TRAINING
Learn the wealth building secrets
of billionaires
(0-07-146661-4)

INSTANT PROFIT
Boost your bottom line with
a cash-building plan
(0-07-146668-1)

SUCCESSFUL FRANCHISING
Learn how to buy or sell a franchise
(0-07-146671-1)

INSTANT ADVERTISING
Create ads that stand out and sell
(0-07-146660-6)

INSTANT REFERRALS
Never cold call or chase after
customers again
(0-07-146667-3)

INSTANT LEADS
Generate a steady flow of leads
(0-07-146663-0)

INSTANT SYSTEMS
Stop running your business and start
growing it
(0-07-146670-3)

INSTANT TEAM BUILDING
Learn the six keys to a winning team
(0-07-146669-X)

*Your source for the strategies, skills,
and confidence every business owner
needs to succeed.*